THE
WAYS
OF
THE WILL

THE
WAYS
OF
THE WILL

*Essays toward a Psychology
and Psychopathology of Will*

LESLIE H. FARBER

Basic Books, Inc., Publishers

NEW YORK / LONDON

To my brother
David J. Farber
1914–1965
WHOSE WILL TO LIVE HEARTENED HIS
FAMILY AND CONFOUNDED HIS PHYSICIANS
ALL HIS YEARS

Preface

Often a man can become absorbed by a radical issue long before he knows its name. At least this is the way that it has been
with me. Twenty-five years ago, I was briefly involved in a
research study of hypnotic dreams, becoming disenchanted
when hypnosis proved to be an unseemly, if not ludicrous,
parody of interhuman possibility. Yet, even after I had abandoned the approach, I continued to be intrigued by the nature
of the hypnotic relationship itself insofar as it was constitutive
of other strange, though ordinary, relationships that by usual
standards could not be called hypnotic. Not, however, until
I came upon an essay on the romantic will by Allen Tate* did
I come to realize that my subject was the problem of will in
human affairs. And, several years later, in the midst of writing
on hysteria, I had the good fortune to spend a few weeks with
Martin Buber, when he came to Washington in 1957 to give
The William Alanson White Memorial Lectures for the Washington School of Psychiatry. One evening, as we walked to the
lecture hall, I idly asked him what he thought the future held
for psychoanalysis or for psychotherapy in general. To my
surprise, since he could not have known of my own preoccupation, he replied that he believed my profession needed
more than anything else for its further development a psy-

* "Three Types of Poetry," *On the Limits of Poetry* (New York:
The Swallow Press and William Morrow and Co., 1948).

chology of will. By now we had entered the hall, and there was no chance for me to say that this was precisely the matter that had been concerning me. And neither of us returned subsequently to his remark. Nevertheless, his words encouraged and confirmed my resolve to pursue the problem of a psychology of will, a resolve that has culminated in this book.

There is no need to emphasize here the importance of Buber's theories in the unfolding of my own speculations on the subject of will, since several chapters in this volume are devoted to him. Like many in this country, I find it difficult to think of Buber without at the same time thinking of my good friend Maurice Friedman, who more than any other person has been responsible for the presentation and exegesis of Buber's philosophy in America. Because Professor Friedman is one of the few philosophers sensitive to and knowledgeable about the questions raised by psychotherapy, I have been privileged to seek his counsel, not only about Buber's writings, but on other pressing questions, stemming from the encounter between philosophy and psychology. I shall always be in his debt for his constant generostiy and understanding in the preparation of this book.

I would acknowledge here my appreciation to Marjorie Farber, who for many years gave all manner of literary and philosophical assistance during a time when my ties to the medical aspects of psychotherapy were too recent to be questioned or explored. In particular, I am grateful for her persistence in fostering an affection for the writings of Sören Kierkegaard—an affection that has remained to this day.

There is, of course, no end to the colleagues and students who have contributed to the development of my own theories, but I should like to single out the special contribution of Fr. William F. Lynch. At a time when I was only beginning to investigate the disabilities of will, described in this volume,

Preface

I learned that Father Lynch was simultaneously occupied with the privileges of will—or "wishing," to use his own term—as he formulated a psychology of hope.* Thus, to our mutual pleasure, we discovered that our interests were reciprocal and complementary. Out of our many conversations have come both instruction and friendship, neither really being able to exist without the other.

Finally, allowing for the perfunctory quality attending most marital acknowledgments, I still mean to convey my heartfelt gratitude to my wife, Anne Farber, whose devotion was manifested in countless exertions on behalf of this book. She was always unstinting in her willingness to assist in every task, whether trivial or essential. For such devotion, gratitude is a small word.

LESLIE H. FARBER

Washington, D.C.
February 1966

* Images of Hope (Baltimore-Dublin: Helicon Press, 1965).

Contents

PREFACE vii

1 *Introduction: The Two Realms of Will* 1
2 *Will and Anxiety* 26
3 *I'm Sorry, Dear* 51
4 *Despair and the Life of Suicide* 76
5 *Will and Willfulness in Hysteria* 99
6 *Faces of Envy* 118
7 *Martin Buber and Psychoanalysis* 131
8 *The Therapeutic Despair* 155
9 *Schizophrenia and the Mad Psychotherapist* 184
10 *Perfectibility and the Psychoanalytic Candidate* 209

ACKNOWLEDGMENTS 220

INDEX 221

THE
WAYS
OF
THE WILL

I

INTRODUCTION
THE TWO REALMS
OF WILL

In this introduction, I shall try to make as explicit as possible
the principles contained in my approach to a psychology of
will. The essays that make up this volume were addressed to
particular occasions, and, though they separately examined one
or more aspects of the problem of will, it was my hope that
each essay would in some measure stand alone. But such self-
sufficiency becomes a disadvantage in a book such at this.
Since no attempt has been made to alter the essays, there is an
unavoidable amount of repetition and overlapping which I
trust will not prove tiresome to the reader. Another disadvantage to this method of presentation lies in the facts that each
essay develops its own portion of theory out of the special
problem confronted and that no single essay contains in
entirety all the principles involved in my approach. Though
I shall try to remedy this last deficiency in the course of this
introduction, I am compelled to say, in my own defense, that

the subject of will has never suffered abstraction gladly, proving most elusive when viewed most theoretically—or so it has seemed to me, in both my reading and my writing. I have come to believe increasingly that the vitality of the subject of will depends on an intricate interplay between the general and the concrete. To the extent that I have realized such interplay, principles and phenomena will rely on each other for both their existence and their truth.

Traditionally, will has been the category through which we examine that portion of our life that is the mover of our life in a direction or toward an objective in time. But, like several other important human concerns, its meaning has shifted over and over again according to the cultural, philosophical, political, and religious climate of the time. For the sake of brevity, let me try to represent concretely the variety of meaning attributed to the word "will" through the ages.

My decision here, in the Aristotelian or Scholastic sense of will, is not to attempt a philosophical history of the subject of will, useful as that might be. Since my philosophical scholarship is meager, I would indeed need passion (another manner in which we use the term "will") to pursue, in the face of my limitations, such a deliberately scholarly program. Even so, I must confess my temptation, out of pride or "self-will," to affect the appearance, if not the substance, of scholarship. But, lacking the necessary passion and withstanding my prideful temptations, I would be equally foolish to resort to resolutions about such a course: will power is the name we give to fiats that run counter to our appetites or inclinations. Or, to put the matter somewhat differently, I can safely say that I do not have the will to scholarship, in the way a person may be said to have the will to believe, the will to power, or merely the will to succeed. Though I think that I can usually bring myself to pay my bills each month and to answer some of my correspondence, I do not believe that I can force the scholarly task on myself in an ongoing way. For me it would go against the grain. In fact, I cannot even persuade myself to master the scholarly digestions of others, as they appear in histories of philosophy or even in the *Synopticon* of the Great Books, the latter containing a number of pages of fine-print categories, subcategories, and subsubcategories all relating to the subject of will. Much as I believe that I should be able to do this, inevitably, in the case of the *Synopticon*, I fall into an apathetic state, a sort of Oblomovism, which has been called "will-lessness," during which I succumb to reveries about how Mortimer Adler, sharing my lack of will to scholarship, chose to parcel out works and topics to hungry graduate students. "You say you're doing St. Augustine on sex? I envy you. I've got him on grace." Such parceling, so characteristic of large scientific projects, is one of the ways the will invents in its own image: the task is split into fragments that other wills will find manageable. And, even when the scholarly history is the work of one philosopher, only the most superb artistry can contrive a faithful and meaningful exposition of the thought of all those masters who have written on the subject of will. Anything less would result in mere synopsis or, worse yet, would be an instance of what Yeats called "the will trying to do the work of the imagination." We have too many instances of the ways in which the modern will, in the sense of the prevailing spirit of the times, seeks to digest the great works into small primers or comic books that any man or child can understand. And, if there is a transcendental or divine will to oppose such vulgarizations, it does not make itself clearly heard or felt.

In the preceding passage, then, we have instances of most of the meanings will has acquired since the beginnings of Western philosophy. Though the subject of will has been largely neglected by modern psychology and though it has fallen into relative disrepute in modern formal philosophy, many of these meanings are part of our informal thought and conversation.

Even if it were to disappear altogether from the scholarly disciplines, the subject of will would nevertheless survive as an essential and literal part of our language, that is, in the simple and volitive future tense of verb forms, as well as in the verb "to will." I may simply say, "I shall do this," thereby announcing in moderate tone my intention to perform this act in the future. Besides intention, choice and decision are implied in my statement, insofar as I mean that I shall do this instead of that. Now, if I wish to add determination or resolution to this act, I can shift to the volitive future tense. Rather than saying, "I shall do this," I now say, "I will do this." Through stress, I can further intensify one or several aspects of this anticipated action. If it is the selfhood or self-will of the event that impresses me, I can say, "*I* will do this." To heighten still more the determination already heightened by the volitive future tense, I can say, "I *will* do this." On the other hand, should I be wary that my determination will dwindle into mere resolution without ensuing action, I shall say, "I will *do* this," or even, "I *will do* this." Of course, if I am convinced that it is the rightness of my cause that calls forth my effort, I shall say, without necessarily any gain in modesty, "I will do *this*." To capture all the passion and spirit surrounding this deed, I may choose, in the manner of the romantic poets, to stress the entire statement: "*I will do this!*" However, extravagant stress, or what seems extravagant these days, runs the risk of diminishing the matter to its original unstressed form: "I will do this." In fact, obscurely sensing the hazards of invoking will in such explicit and noisy fashion, I may prefer to underplay the issue, saying merely, "I want to do this," or even, "I think that I would like to do this." There is no need here to develop the possibilities of the verb "to will," because the verb recognizes the substantive topic of will. Besides, the shades of difference between the stressed volitive future tense of "I *will* do this" and "I will to do this" are slight.

4

In summary, then, our everyday language, spoken and written, recapitulates the meanings acquired by the subject of will in philosophical scholarship, although it is more likely that such scholarship recapitulates the meanings of everyday language.

In the essay "Will and Anxiety," there is some consideration of the reasons the subject of will fell into disfavor in philosophy and the reasons the new psychological sciences—particularly psychoanalysis—developed without explicit recourse to the matter of will. In this same essay, I have tried to assess the penalties incurred by psychology through repudiating the will as responsible mover and turning instead to various motives and drives, largely irresponsible, that were then asked to do the work of the will.

Because he would seem to be the exception, some mention must be made here of Otto Rank, whose "will psychology" and "will therapy" flourished for a time in psychology. His conception of will was derived almost wholly from Nietzsche, whom he esteemed as "the first . . . and up to now the only psychologist."[1] Rank regarded will as a life force, muffled and dampened by the moralities of religion that reduced man to guilt and impotence. To him, the ideas of Freud and Adler were as blameworthy as religion in their "moral evaluation" of the will as "bad," aiming not at liberation, but at further subjugation of the will—as opposed to Nietzsche, who was "the first and only one who could affirm the evil will."[2] Thus, Rank urged that

individual psychology . . . refrain from moral evaluation of every kind. It is important that the neurotic above all learn to will, discover that he can will without getting guilt feeling on account of willing. . . . Purely psychological consideration would show that

[1] Otto Rank, *Will Therapy and Truth and Reality* (New York: Alfred A. Knopf, 1950), p. 226.
[2] *Ibid.*, p. 226.

it is his own inner inhibitions that make the individual not only moral but even hyperethical.[3]

In contrast with my own approach, not to mention most classical scholarship, Rank saw religion and morality as adversaries of the will. His reasoning resembles that of Kirillov in Dostoyevsky's *The Possessed*, who argued, just before his suicide, that man "has hitherto been so unhappy and so poor because he has been afraid to assert his will in the highest point and has shown his self-will only in little things, like a schoolboy." (See "Despair and the Life of Suicide.") In a sense, Rank's will is the familiar romantic will, whose object is the assertion of personal singularity or individuality and whose hazard is megalomania, if the claims of guilt and despair are evaded.

Despite his wish to found a psychology of will, Otto Rank is now remembered for certain technical strategies that characterized his "will therapy"—strategies designed to train the will to pursue its way without the burden of guilt. He summarized the stages of will therapy in this manner:

The first developmental phase of the individual will, as it manifests itself in counter-will, corresponds to a "not willing," because one must; the second phase, that of positive will expression, corresponds to a "willing" what one must; the third creative phase, to a willing of that which one wants.[4]

In psychoanalysis, according to Rank, the patient responds to the analyst's will with his own "counter-will." He found it unfortunate that psychoanalysis evaluated this protest morally as "resistance," which had to be dispelled through examination of the transference, thus failing to utilize "the actual therapeutic value" contained in this expression of "counter-will." "The goal of constructive therapy is not the overcoming of

[3] *Ibid.*, p. 9.
[4] *Ibid.*, p. 299.

resistance but the transformation of the negative will expression (counter-will) . . . into positive and eventually creative expression."[5] His principal device for achieving this transformation was what he called "end-setting." If I am not mistaken, "counter-will" is jargon for what we more commonly call "willfulness." (See "Will and Willfulness in Hysteria.") "End-setting" means diverting willfulness, whether it consists of an indiscriminate "no" or an indiscriminate "yes," to more feasible, if not more utilitarian, goals. In moral terms, this strategy could be seen as an exercise in humility, depending not only on the feasibility, but also on the nature and relevance of the goals chosen.

In summary, then, the Nietzschean will, proposed by Otto Rank, bears little resemblance to my own conception of will. I would further identify Rank's "counter-will" as "willfulness," which is only one of the more hysterical forms of will's many disabilities.

In a general way, as I mentioned earlier, will is the category through which we examine that portion of our life that is the mover of our life in a certain direction or toward an objective in time. But, this general statement must now give way to a distinction between two different realms of will. This distinction, I should add, is intended to be a phenomenological, rather than a moral or religious one, which is to say, the goal of the will in either realm may range from mere physical exertion to a serious decision that influences the course of an entire life. Thus, these two realms must not be understood as a gnostic division of life into the ideal and the trivial, the religious and the secular, or the perfect and the imperfect.

In the first realm, will itself is not a matter of experience, though its presence may be retrospectively inferred *after* this realm has given way. When no longer in the first realm, I may

[5] *Ibid.*, p. 19.

7

arbitrarily say of a given enterprise that I willed or wished its fulfillment with all my might and heart, meaning that, at this later moment, I abstract will from the event in an attempt to portray both mover and movement. With equal justification, I might discuss, once I am outside the first realm of will, my enterprise in terms of passion, discrimination, intelligence, intention, responsibility, or even irresponsibility, knowing the abstraction I chose does poor justice to the totality of the first realm, in which will is joined to all appropriate human capacities—mental and physical, intellectual and emotional—to form a seamless whole enclosing me that pushes in a particular direction at the same time that the direction in the world enlists my will and the faculties wedded to it. Perhaps W. H. Auden had something similar in mind, when he wrote in *The Dyer's Hand:*

All the existentialist descriptions of choice, like Pascal's wager or Kierkegaard's leap, are interesting as dramatic literature, but are they true? When I look back at the three or four choices in my life which have been decisive, I find that, at the time I made them, I had very little sense of the seriousness of what I was doing and only later did I discover what had seemed an unimportant brook was, in fact, a Rubicon.[6]

Since it is not a matter of immediate experience and must be inferred after the event, will of the first realm may be said to be unconscious.[7] When Auden writes that, at the time of

---

[6] W. H. Auden, *The Dyer's Hand* (New York: Random House, 1962), p. 103.

[7] My use of "unconscious," whether as adjective or noun, derives from remarks by Martin Buber in a seminar in Washington, D.C., in 1957. The unconscious, as I understand him, is that state that precedes the split into psychical and physical, both being radically different modes of knowing that exist in consciousness. Buber would say, I think, that the unconscious is being itself, and that the physical and psychical are evolving out of it again and again at every moment. Seen in this way, the dream that I formulate on waking is a conscious psychical statement about dreaming itself, which was prior to the evolvement of

8

decision, he had "very little sense of the seriousness" of what he was doing, I understand him to say that he was not conscious of the place of will. His statement is understandably compressed. But, I would assume he would not really confine his decision to one instantaneous, or even prolonged, flash of enlightenment or revelation: it was no doubt extended in time and replete with all those worldly activities that belong to every decision. Moreover, I would assume there were periods, outside the first realm of will, when he was painfully conscious of the seriousness of his move, when he attempted some rational assessment of the advantages and disadvantages of his decision, and when he was often reduced to pushing laboriously from one task to another. Such conscious and self-conscious periods would belong to the second realm of will, which I shall discuss shortly.

The first realm of will moves in a direction, rather than toward a particular object. Direction, here, is to be understood, not as an ideal goal toward which we press, however much we falter, but rather as a way interspersed with, yet not obstructed by, worldly detail and worldly objectives. Direction, therefore, is a way whose end cannot be known—a way open to possibility, including the possibility of failure. While this realm must, to some degree, remain impenetrable to inspection, its predominant experience is one of freedom—the

---

the psychic and physical. In relation to will, the ruminations about the seriousness of decision and much of the associated bodily effort in the world are conscious psychical and physical aspects of the second realm of will. When Buber surveyed the vast history of philosophical speculation about the unconscious, he found nothing to improve on Plotinus, who wrote in the third century: "For it is very possible that even without being conscious of having something one has it in himself and even in a form more effective than if he knew it. . . . Consciousness seems to obscure the actions it perceives, and only when they occur without it are they purer, more effective, more vital" (Buber's translation; see equivalent passage in Stephen MacKenna, trans., Plotinus, *The Enneads* [New York: Pantheon Books, 1957], p. 290).

freedom to think, speak, and act forthrightly and responsibly, without blinking the hazards such freedom entails. In traditional theory, "free will" implies an irreducible will that may freely choose a particular course with all measure of responsibility. But, the freedom experienced in the first realm is more immediate and anterior than any philosophical, legal, or political freedom we may speculate about, once we have left that realm. All other freedoms are derivative of, or grounded in, the freedom of the first realm. Moreover, I suspect that much of the speculation about freedom and will, particularly of the Aristotelian or Scholastic variety, stems from our necessary, and often irresistible, effort to give rational or ethical form to this freedom. No matter how intricate and valuable these speculations may become, they inevitably fail to capture the totality of the first realm, just as telling a dream can never encompass dreaming itself.

Despite some resemblance in terms of wholeness, transience, and forthrightness, this first realm is not the same as the relation called "I–thou." As a realm of movement or action, no relation need occur within it, even though relation is always a dialogic potentiality. While it could be said that this realm could not exist without the shadow and hope of "I–thou," it is also true that "I–thou" increasingly requires the first realm of will for its realization. A lively reciprocity between will and relation reveals itself early and persists for the remainder of life. Through most of his first year of life, the child lives wholly in relation and wholly out of relation, which is to say that, when relation is interrupted, he screams at his loss until relation is restored. But, toward the end of his first year, he ventures away from relation toward the objects and skills that will increasingly occupy his world, such ventures becoming a passionate, often stubborn, manifestation of his burgeoning will. At this point, the reciprocity between will and relation is striking: relation may be suspended, or held in abeyance, or actively spurned, as his will finds its way. And, on occasion, the child, as well as his parents, can be seen trying to force will to do the work of relation, or to force relation to do the work of the will, both extremes representing early infringements of both relation and the first realm of will—infringements that must be contended with, in varying degree, for the remainder of life.

As might be anticipated, it is the second realm of will that more readily permits direct phenomenological and psychological exploration. The will of this realm, being conscious, need not be inferred after the fact, but is *experienced during* the event. No longer an abstraction, will's singularity in this realm can be as obtrusive as my own arm, or my own rage, and its thrust is experienced by me as will. I may invoke its assistance, or its tyranny may defeat me, but in either case—as friend or foe—I can distinguish its presence. Unlike the joined totality of the first realm, the course of the will in this realm is relatively isolated, the degree of isolation depending on the matter being willed and the faculties supporting, or opposing, this willing. Since this will presses toward a particular objective—rather than a direction, as in the first realm—it can be said, roughly speaking, to be utilitarian in character: I do this to get that, which has its utility, which in turn can be important, trivial, or even harmful. In other words, the end of the will's exertion is anticipated to some degree before I begin: I learn algebra to pass my algebra test, to graduate from high school, to enter college, to win a college diploma, and so on. Obviously, life contains a vast variety of getting, achieving, winning, possessing, doing, and owning that is responsive to this will. Some of these objectives, when reached, may turn out to have little utility, while the direction of the will of the first realm may have great utility, though utility is neither its motive nor its purpose. At any rate, the face of the object willed by will of the second realm is known in some fashion from the beginning, and therefore there is a discrete, tangible, visible, and temporal end to the willing of this realm. We have only to think of our schooling, which most of us endure under some duress, to see a profusion of items, useful and useless, which we have acquired over the years through this will. At the same time, it is important to stress that there is no accomplishment, distinction, skill, task, or reward that cannot lose its discrete quality when this will gives way, as it must, over and over, to the first realm of will, there to merge into the flow in a given direction.

Before we become lost in a swamp of generalizations, let me try to illustrate these two realms of will with a passage from Tolstoy's *Anna Karenina,* describing the vicissitudes of decision in the lives of Koznyshev and Varenka when they are accidentally thrown together during a visit to Levin's and Kitty's estate in the country. Koznyshev, Levin's half-brother, is a middle-aged, scholarly fellow, who had one unhappy love affair early in his life with a girl named Marie, but ever since has been a confirmed bachelor. Varenka, Kitty's friend, is a spinster, rather masculine in appearance, with a charming deep voice. She, too, has more or less given up the possibility of marriage for herself. But, in the course of this visit, she and Koznyshev are drawn to each other, and both of them now wonder if at long last marriage isn't a real possibility. On this particular day, Varenka offers to take the children of the estate out into the woods to hunt for mushrooms. Koznyshev, whose habits are usually sedentary, insists on accompanying her and the children, and with this gesture both of them know that the moment is at hand. Koznyshev has already convinced himself that Varenka would be an ideal mate, that he would not thus betray the memory of his youthful love, Marie. He has even rehearsed his proposal and decided to himself, on the basis of obvious signs, that Varenka would respond favorably. After a while, the two of them move away from the children who are scurrying for mushrooms, and now they have the privacy they have been hoping for. I quote from Tolstoy:

They walked a few steps in silence. Varenka saw that he wanted to speak; she guessed what it was about and grew faint with joy and fear. They had gone so far that they could not be overheard by anyone, but still he did not speak. Varenka would have done better not to break the silence, for after a silence it would have been easier for them to say what they wanted to say than after talking about mushrooms; but almost against her will, almost by accident, Varenka said:

"So you haven't found anything? But then of course there are always fewer in the middle of the wood."

Koznyshev heaved a sigh and made no answer. He was vexed that she should have spoken about the mushrooms. He wanted to bring her back to her first remark about her childhood; but as though against his own will, after a longish pause, he made a remark in reply to her last words.

"I've only heard that white mushrooms grow mostly at the edge of the woods, though I can't tell which are the white ones."

A few more minutes passed; they had gone still farther from the children and were quite alone. Varenka's heart was thumping so hard that she could hear it and she felt herself turning red, then pale, then red again.

To be the wife of a man like Koznyshev . . . seemed to her the height of happiness. Besides, she was almost sure she was in love with him. And now in another moment it had to be decided. She was terrified. Terrified of what he might and what he might not say.

Now or never was the moment when he had to make their position clear; Koznyshev, too, felt this. Everything about Varenka —her look, her blush, her lowered eyes—showed that she was in a state of painful suspense. Koznyshev saw it and was sorry for her. He even felt that to say nothing now would be to offend her. He quickly went over in his mind all the arguments in favor of his decision. He repeated to himself the words in which he had intended to propose to her. But instead of those words, by some sort of unaccountable idea that came into his mind, he suddenly asked:

"What is the difference between a white and a birch mushroom?"

Varenka's lips trembled with agitation when she replied: "There is hardly any difference in the cap. It's the stalks that are different."

And the moment those words were uttered, both he and she understood that it was all over, that what should have been said would never be said, and their agitation, having reached its climax, began to subside.

"The stalk of a birch mushroom," said Koznyshev, who had completely regained his composure, "reminds me of the stubble on the chin of a dark man who has not shaved for two days."

"Yes, that's true," Varenka replied with a smile, and involuntarily the direction of their walk changed. They began walking toward the children. Varenka felt hurt and ashamed, but at the same time she experienced a sense of relief.

When he got home and went over his reasons again, Koznyshev came to the conclusion that his first decision had been wrong. He could not be unfaithful to the memory of Marie.[8]

In spite of their conscious will to consummate their longings into a clear proposal of marriage, Varenka and Koznyshev both will to do otherwise in a manner in which they are not even conscious of willing. Approaching their memory of privacy, both are apprehensive and self-conscious, both wholly absorbed with those few words which, when spoken, will constitute a proposal: he has rehearsed his overture, she her acceptance. Yet, every time they are on the verge of addressing each other, they find themselves skittering away. Within the second realm of will, they only know what they have determined to do, and, in this bondage, they are no longer capable of imagining the other or even of understanding how they have arrived at this particular moment. So Koznyshev is reduced to repeating to himself the words he had intended to use, and Varenka to hearing her heart pounding, feeling her-

[8] Leo Tolstoy, *Anna Karenina* (New York: The New American Library, 1961), pp. 565–566.

self turn red, then pale, then red again. And then, "unaccounta-
bly" and "almost against their will," they discover themselves
talking about mushrooms instead of marriage. Almost immediately they realize that they have jointly repudiated marriage, and this repudiation now seems right to them. It is worth
noting here that Tolstoy scrupulously resists invading the
totality of this moment. Later, Koznyshev decides he could
not be unfaithful to his memory of Marie. And, perhaps in a
few years, he will explain to friends how his memory of Marie
protected him from a foolish temptation. More likely, though,
Koznyshev and Varenka, over the years, will return again and
again to this decision, wondering how it reflected their aspirations, needs, and temperaments, and, very possibly, they will
wonder how much of this searching entered into that opaque
moment whose totality will ever elude them.

The problem of will lies in our recurring temptation to
apply the will of the second realm to those portions of life
that not only will not comply, but that will become distorted
under such coercion. Let me give a few examples: I can will
knowledge, but not wisdom; going to bed, but not sleeping;
eating, but not hunger; meekness, but not humility; scrupu-
losity, but not virtue; self-assertion or bravado, but not
courage; lust, but not love; commiseration, but not sympathy;
congratulations, but not admiration; religiosity, but not faith;
reading, but not understanding. The list could be extended,
but it must be clear, when will of the second realm turns to
such qualities, that it seeks in its utilitarian way to capture
through imitation their public face—the manner or style that
is visible and objective, as well as available.

I can will speech or silence, but not conversation. Leaving
the great decisions of life, let us turn now to the ordinary issue
of speaking and listening. As a case in point, let us consider the
friend whose besetting sin it is to overpower or monopolize

almost every conversation he enters. After the event, he is likely to berate himself for having once again been noisy and obtuse and, in the spirit of contrition, may resolve to hold his peace on the next occasion. Providing he does not will recollection,[9] like a man bent on recovering a name which has

[9] The antagonism between memory and will of the second realm has an important place in those disorders called obsessional—disorders largely characterized by the will to be conscious, or even rational, about all manner of mental and physical detail. The will to be conscious includes the will to be consciously moral that is accompanied by the suspicion of immorality in all matters unconscious. Fearing that he may leave the gas jets on and asphyxiate himself and others, the victim of such a disorder finds himself unable to recall his precise movements in turning the gas jets off. In fact, as his memory falters in the face of his will to remember, he may wonder whether he neglected altogether to turn off one or more jets. In this manner, he persuades himself to try the jets again; at the same time, he cautions himself to be watchful enough of his efforts so that when he leaves the stove he will be able to remember, or know for certain, that the jets, once and for all, are safely turned off. But when he returns from the stove and wills himself to remember this event, memory again flees the will's demands, and he is driven to try the jets again. As the opposition between will and memory becomes more obsessive and circumscribed, the humiliating drama described above must be re-enacted within the narrow confines of stove and jets. After checking one jet and then starting to check another, he can no longer will an exact recollection of what he did with the first jet; he is no longer sure whether consciousness of his physical effort may not have lapsed for a moment. One of his more agonizing, if not futile, tasks is to prevent his conscious will from "lapsing" into the first realm of will, in which will is unconscious. So he must return to the first jet, perhaps this time resolving to try the jet five times in order to allow for such lapses. However, memory of his counting may elude him as much as his physical movements: did he or did he not skip the third check? Or, on the other hand, did he perform the third check twice? By now the obligation to total memory is absolute, so that exactly five checks—no more, no less—are as necessary as safety itself. At this stage, qualities such as imagination hardly exist, his will doing what work there is to be done. Should he try to consider the mechanical reliability of the jets, instead of imagining this real possibility, he wills a certainty of knowledge about the mechanism which cannot be had. Ultimately, and not too fancifully, these jets will seem to have a perverse will of their

passed out of mind, he may slowly and remorsefully return in memory to the evening and, potentially at least, recapture most of his chattering. Probably his memory will be precise in that other people and their words now appear as indistinct and unconvincing as they appeared during the evening itself. If he has the strength, he may critically assess his repetitions, his didacticism and contentiousness, and even imagine now what should have been said—or, better yet, left unsaid. Nevertheless, the next occasion may unfortunately provide that familiar incendiary instant in which his resolve not to talk gives way to his insistence on having his full say. Should an embarrassed mate try to remind him of his previous resolution, he will heatedly argue that this occasion is different, the issue larger, and that courage demands his speaking long and loud. From the standpoint of his own experience, he will passionately regard himself as being all of a piece—a creature of heart and substance. His earlier resolution will now seem to have been born of timidity, if he can bring himself to consider it at all, which is doubtful. Within this rush of will to speak, which belongs to the second realm of will just as much as his previous resolution not to speak, both memory and imagination shrink, when compared with the acuity of his time of contrition. Thus, if his mate persists, he can perhaps recall the resolution itself, but his memory can no longer retrieve those memories and imaginative discriminations that first led him to make his resolution. In other words, his resolution, even if he should recall it, stands thin and arbitrary and irrelevant, now that it is deprived of memory and imagination. No longer does it deserve his respect and obedience. Of course, once the evening

---

own—a will not to turn off in the face of his determination to turn them off. Thus does it happen that people are stalled for unconscionable stretches of time—turning off stoves, locking doors, adding columns of figures, washing and rewashing themselves—simply because memory will not yield to will of the second realm.

is over and the rush of will subsides, shame over his new excesses will return, making him wonder why it is so difficult for him to will himself not to speak. And, as he painfully begins to inspect his new conversational failure, he will quickly abandon his subjective certainty that his display belonged, in effect, to the first realm of will—that realm in which one decides without knowing a decision has taken place.

It would be unfair, at this point, not to mention the friend whose habitual sin in conversation is one of enforced silence. In his nights of contrition, he replays those episodes when he wished to speak and would not, when caution born of pride made him swallow not his pride but his words. During remorse, his silence, or his will not to talk, seems to him as self-indulgent as the noise produced by our talkative friend. If he resists willing his recall of the unpleasant evening and denies himself the solace of defending his silence as an act of modesty, he may come to view some of the many ways in which his silence served neither him nor the conversation, being at times as mindless and cruel as a vindictive monologue. It will always be tempting to interrupt this critical inspection with large resolutions to talk on the next social occasion. Needless to say, there are resolutions and resolutions. On the one hand, a resolution may be a concise statement of intention whose provenance is the first realm of will; on the other hand, a resolution may be no more than a hollow and ineffectual assertion about the future, with the added burden that it serves to defeat the possibilities belonging to the first realm. But, if he can return again and again to his scrutiny, he may now begin to imagine where being forthright, rather than mute, might not only have been kinder, but might have provided the conditions for listening. Having come this far, he may now regard such self-conscious resolutions—whether to speak or not to speak— as altogether beside the point. Still, as often happens, when the new moment arrives in its own surprising way, he may not be equal to it. Should his well-meaning mate remind him that he does have an opinion about the subject at hand, he will characteristically deny the importance of any opinion he might have, forgetting that with this denial he has already begun to will silence. Although his mate cannot know this, the fact may be that in his absorption with his will to talk, he has not really followed the conversation and, as a consequence, may have no opinion. No doubt, he too will reach for the consolation, however fictitious, that his self-imposed silence was an eloquent response to this particular conversation.

I have suggested that, out of shame, both our friends eventually reconsider their excesses by appealing to memory and imagination—capacities which failed them badly during the occasion itself. Unfortunately, my account has contained the hint that each sinner witnesses in remorse a pageant of his misdeeds that allows him, if not conversion to a new way, at least more circumspection. Let me dispel this melodramatic notion. If our friends evade all the distractions and resolutions that would put the matter out of mind, their various ways of reconstructing and confronting their misbehavior may still belong to the second realm of will. One friend may resolutely wish to know all that he said and did; and where his memory fails him, his mate will supply the missing information. In time, he may recapture the entire literal script: every "he said" and "I said" and "I failed to say" in its chronological place. Memory here has compiled a recapitulation of a past event, which, like other eye-witness descriptions or verbatim reports, still requires, for the sake of meaning, a feat of imaginative discrimination that may or may not come. Our other friend's memory, since he is of another temperament, may be more emotional than literal, making up in heat what it lacks in verbal detail. As an aesthetic rendering, it may loudly announce the ugliness of his performance, without necessarily making the moral discriminations which would be appropriate. (See "Will and Willfulness in Hysteria.") I would stress that both memories are bound to an evening in the past, much as the will of the second realm is bound to a distinct object or goal in the future. Also, I would stress that both memories are separated, though not divorced, from imagination.

Whether focused on specific happenings in the past or extended forward to specific happenings in the future, imagination too may be subject to the second realm of will. If our friends, on the basis of past history, do not disqualify themselves absolutely from further social evenings, very likely their imaginings will be attempts to shape a particular encounter in the future. After all, from their distance, what can they really anticipate about the next social gathering? A group of people talking: vocal noise whose meaning cannot be determined in advance. They can caution themselves to drink or not to drink, leave early, observe the amenities, avoid certain people and certain subjects. But none of these imaginings will ensure imagination when the moment arrives. Fearing that his anticipations betray a failure of imagination, our friend may ask his mate to perform the imaginative or critical task. Unhappily, unless his imagination can respond in kind, marital solicitude will be heard as coercion. Whether his sin has been silence or jabbering, he may try to imagine himself listening, and then responding or not responding, depending on what is said. But, an important quality of imagination, in the best sense, is imagining imagination's limits. And, what the other person will say must to some degree remain unimaginable, if we are to reply imaginatively when he actually speaks. To the extent that we can predict what another will say, no dialogue will occur. As far as our two friends are concerned, all they have been able to predict thus far has been their own conversational disasters. In "Martin Buber and Psychoanalysis," I have suggested that listening requires something more than remaining mute while looking attentive—namely, it requires the ability to attend imaginatively to another's language. Actually, in listening we speak the other's words. It is not merely that listening does not respond to the constraints we impose, but that it withers as human possibility under will's dominion, as all of us realize who have tried to force our attention to an event, while our inclination struggled to look elsewhere.

Since we can assume our friends do not live entirely through the second realm of will, we must now, in order to do them justice, make inferences about memory and imagination as they occur within the first realm of will, realizing, of course, that these inferences can hardly capture that realm's totality. To begin with, memory and imagination can be separated only arbitrarily, for within the first realm each requires the other for its vitality: memory is necessarily an imaginative venture; imagination draws upon memory for its historical reality. The most important statement that can be made about memory and imagination is that in their movements they are *constitutive*. They are constitutive of who we were and are and would be, as well as the ways in which we fail at this private mission. Though no single effort may encompass all these possibilities, at least this is their direction. Considered in this manner, memory and imagination may be understood to have a preponderantly moral dimension, surveying how we succeed or fail to realize our own particular human potentiality and, equally urgent, how we fulfill or betray the human order. Being constitutive, memory and imagination are not literal and therefore do not have to recapitulate every fragment of an experience. But, this is not to say that they will not expand their achievements with literal contributions from the second realm. A constitutive event is an actual past happening, not fabrication, which gains ever new meaning with the passage of time through accretion, as personal history unfolds—at the same time that the happening and its accretions affect the unfolding. It is the genius of memory to discover the event and the genius of imagination to pursue its reflections in the ensuing life. Obviously, it is impossible to know whether what we are now living through will, in time, become constitutive in the eyes of memory and imagination, for what seems remarkable now may become trivial, and what seems unremarkable now may become constitutive. This is the process which enables us to say of a past occurrence that it revealed our particular concerns even then, but that we could not know them at the time. Recalling the unpleasantness of the previous evening, our two friends may fasten on one of the evening's more enigmatic, yet surprising, moments, then drift back in time to another moment, more revealing than enigmatic, which in turn enlightens or calls into question a future possibility. But, should they now try consciously to remember these constitutive movements of memory and imagination, their memory will resemble, in its gaps and distortions, the dream they tell on waking, rather than the dream they actually dreamed.

Memory and imagination within the first realm of will, I would emphasize, share in that realm's dialogic potentiality. In fact, even in solitude these capacities seem to move in the direction of another human being. However, it is just as possible that left to their own devices, our two friends might very well be restricted to the literal boundaries of the second realm. To some extent, it is guilt which makes them turn to their mates—for comfort, if not for enlightenment. But, their turning may also come from their faith that out of real talk, as opposed to monologic silence or monologic chatter, memories and imaginings, with their attendant discriminations, will arise that, in solitude, could not be anticipated.

But, is it only activity of such a relatively high human order, as speaking and listening, that resists the will of the second realm? Let us assume that our two friends, despairing over their record of social failure and their inability to contend with that failure imaginatively, now anticipate the approaching party with foreboding and dread—dread that still another catastrophe awaits them. Even as they are resolving to speak or not to speak, their separate wills invade their ordinary worlds in a peculiarly disruptive fashion: the familiar and usually thoughtless routine of preparation—washing, shaving, dressing, arranging, driving—now disintegrates, shattering into unwieldy fragments, each of which must be separately and arduously pulled into place. All that is usually taken for granted in social life is now transformed into a disheartening series of tiring mental and physical tasks—each task requiring, with mounting fatigue, a new effort of will. Even the preliminary phone call, through which our guests check time and route with their host, splinters under will's impact into the labors of finding the number in the directory, and asking and writing directions.

This is the rough terrain on which the nag insists we join him as he worries us with what we should have done and failed to do, or what we did and should have done differently. It would be inaccurate to call this terrain a world in which we live, because it exists outside us as the adversary or accomplice of our wills. Procrastination, in this connection, can be seen as forfeiture or postponement of action on this terrain that has been created by the will. Distraction, still in the same connection, would be the will's way of inventing a more pleasant, though transitory, terrain for the will's activities, which—briefly, at least—will serve as illusion for the world that has been lost or replaced.

But, before we continue with the hardships of life on this terrain, once it has become a more or less permanent residence, let us return to the splintering of ordinary affairs that befell our friends as they approached the party of the evening. All of us, I believe, have to contend in some measure with this terrain—some more than others. And now, a distinction must be made. Though the tasks of preparation to which our friends must turn their wills are difficult, they are, nevertheless, possible. This is to say that washing, shaving, and dressing are possible ventures for the isolated will of the second realm, while speaking and listening are not. And, if we look at the work we do, not to mention much of the leisure we create, we can figuratively discern that portion we can do, regardless of interest or wish, and that portion which will not yield to the force of our will and must therefore wait upon the will of the first realm. As I have indicated earlier, when we move —in inspiration, mutuality, or affection—to the first realm, all those items which have yielded their goods are not left behind but enter into the totality of the first realm.

What can we say of the experience of the man who turns for help to his will to achieve those qualities of being that cannot be achieved, or even approached, by means of will? How does his enterprise seem to him? After all, life is profligate in providing occasions which question his attainment and assault his pride. So, it is not as though he were entirely deceived by his will. Unless he is utterly mad, he cannot escape some sense, however dim, of his fraudulence. If he is preoccupied with morality, his preoccupation is apt to be obsessive and, to some degree, related to the shadowy perception of his fraudulence, even though this connection may gradually elude him. To the degree that he is victimized by his will—that is, to the degree that he continues to will what cannot or should not be willed —he will answer challenges to his virtue with the same will that created his predicament. I mentioned earlier, in describing our friends, their inability "to contend imaginatively" with their social failure, their pride, and their shame. Such contention might very well have slowly delineated a moral dilemma, whose delineation was more important than any self-imposed solution. It could even be, though this is not the only conceivable outcome, that their dilemma led them to refuse this party altogether. But, for our imaginatively incapacitated friends, a predicament that had arisen out of will seemed clearly to call for the further intervention of will to effect a solution. Such an endeavor Yeats described as "the will trying to do the work of the imagination." But, the will is unable to imagine; all it really knows in the second realm is how to will. Having no notion of how to "contend imaginatively"

24

with a problem, or even in what way such a response surpasses in quality anything it might devise, will, when summoned to solve some dilemma, conceives the conflict in terms of will and then proposes a solution that consists of one or more wills performing certain tasks—so designed that the solution to the problem rests on their achievement. And so our friends, habitually guided by will, automatically resorted in their predicament to further exertions of will. My answer, then, to the question, what is the nature of the experience of the man who seeks to purchase with his will some semblance of those qualities of being that cannot or should not be willed, is that eventually it is will itself that increasingly becomes his experience, until the private voice of subjectivity and the public occasions from life that might raise this voice are almost stifled, if not silenced. To put the matter somewhat differently, *what is* in his experience gives way to *what should be*, as decreed by his will. One of the more debilitating aspects of his experience, as both subjectivity and the world fade, is the occasional suspicion that troubles him when his will is somnolent: namely, that precisely those powers that cannot or should not be willed are becoming atrophied.

In distinguishing between the two realms of will, I trust I have made it quite clear that the realms are interdependent, that any attempt to develop a theory exclusively from one realm or from the other will end, either in a mysticism which quite betrays the appropriate objectifications the will is capable of, or else in a rationalism that betrays the realities of the wholeness that makes existence possible. With the exception of a few saints of almost unimaginable wholeness and many mad men whose total consistency has rendered them unfit for human company, the majority of us will try to make the best of both realms. We can confidently expect that to the degree the will of the second realm is misshapen, misapplied, or misdirected, the first realm will elude us, even as we willfully assert our proprietary claims over it.

2

WILL
AND
ANXIETY

The last half-century has been a propitious one for the development of psychological theory, particularly for that of the psychoanalytic variety. Without this development, our preoccupation with anxiety would be inconceivable, however impressed we might be by the peculiarly disruptive nature of our present human predicament. It is modern psychology that has given the term "anxiety" a categorical density it never previously carried. Perhaps there is an apprehensive quality characterizing our age that requires the term to be isolated and then weighted—or even exalted—in our vocabulary. Or it may be that we turn in a special way to such a theme as anxiety because our psychological theories, despite the many novel notions they have provided about man's character, deny us other approaches that might be more illuminating. A young movement often must be parochial and even shun traditional knowledge if it is to maintain the enthusiasm necessary for pursuing its inspirations. This is why we counsel the young writer to have his own full say before he resorts to bibliography. But youthful parochialism willfully extended beyond its natural time—that is, shunning every possibility of eventual reconciliation with previous thought—brings a premature senility to the movement, which now enshrines rather than extends its early achievements.

If some detachment is possible, now that our youth draws to a close, I think it can be said the psychological theories that support and derive from psychotherapy have proliferated without explicit recourse to the subject of will, with its vast philosophical and theological literature. Will has been the category through which we examine that portion of our life that is the mover of our life. Though man is ceaselessly subjected to a variety of forces, human and nonhuman, the traditional concept of will asserts that, alone among these many movers, man's power of volition—however frustrated, however often vanquished—is nonetheless accountable, both in achievement and intention. To speak plainly, it is a serious deficiency in our theories that they contain no notion of a responsible mover as it has been described, at its best, since the beginnings of Western history. But, at this point, it may be of historical interest to recall the manner in which Freud turned aside from the category of will in one of his first essays. When Dora—to Freud's great chagrin—unexpectedly terminated treatment after only a few weeks, at a point when his therapeutic ambitions were at their highest, he wrote, after his outrage had subsided, that he recognized one of the limits to psychotherapeutic influence to be the patient's own "will and understanding."[1] But, in the course of this essay, he had second thoughts about his therapeutic failure—thoughts about the nature of transference, which now seemed a more reveal-

[1] Sigmund Freud, "Fragment of an Analysis of a Case of Hysteria," *Collected Papers* (New York: Basic Books, 1959), III, 131.

ing way to understand Dora's interruption of treatment. With this step, Freud may be said to have abandoned the traditional will as a psychological consideration and instead now found, not unlike Schopenhauer, his mover in the libido. Like many important theoretical principles, transference had both advantages and limitations. But, at this date, it should be possible, without demeaning the knowledge gained through transference theory, to consider the price we pay for excluding will from our psychologies.

One reason for that exclusion was that the pioneers in psychotherapy at the turn of the century came largely from the medical sciences, so it is understandable that they would be more taken by the scientific spirit of the time than by the subject of will, with its roots in philosophy and theology— occupations that Freud (and he was not un-typical) regarded as, if not curable, at least arrestable once their pathology was identified. Far more exciting were the discoveries in chemistry, biology, physics, and anthropology. Still, this is only part of the story and really fails to explain, not only why we have no psychology of will, but also why the subject of will fell into general disrepute, even in philosophy, which had proudly fostered it for so many centuries. As could be expected, science and scientific philosophy were antagonistic to the tangled metaphysical speculations on will. And it must be admitted that the antagonism was to some extent earned; much that had been called will badly needed the psychological surgery that psychoanalysis was more than ready to offer. If this readiness seems brash or presumptuous today, we should recall the intoxicating conviction shared by the early leaders of the young movement that there was nothing in all of human history—and especially prehistory—which would not yield to the new psychoanalytic weapons. In this regard, the argument has been made, with considerable generosity, that will was not excluded; that is, by omission or *in absentia*, will *is* the principal, though invisible, actor in the psychoanalytic drama. In other words, will is the residue, like Leonardo da Vinci's genius, remaining after psychoanalytic reduction. Thus, so the argument goes, psychoanalysis serves the purpose of clearing away the brush over-growing the subject of will these many years.

At least some of the responsibility for the will's disfavor, as suggested above, must be credited to the accumulated scholarship on the subject—scholarship which, with certain bright exceptions, is often so tedious as to be virtually unreadable. But tedium alone, I am afraid, would be an insufficient obstacle, to judge from the fashionable careers of other large issues. Even a cursory inspection of this scholarship will reveal that on the one hand the topic of will has been endlessly exploited for all manner of self-serving moralizing and on the other hand came increasingly to be the speculative plaything of the academicians who tinkered with it so whimsically it would be difficult for the reader to know that will had any relevance to human considerations. Thus, either as an ingredient of moral coercion or as a fruitless venture in philosophical or theological academicism, the subject of will gradually lost its connection with existence itself. On this basis alone, it is understandable why the psychotherapists at the beginning of the century preferred to abandon—or rather bury—this bloodless category. They would have needed both patience and erudition to root out the exceptions to this dreariness—the extraordinary thinkers who grasped the anthropological necessity for the term "will." Whichever emphasis they gave the will—choice, decision, resolution, passion, intention, determination, or spirit—these exceptional men tried at best to preserve will's identity as responsible mover, whether that mover be individual, communal, or divine. And they had assistance here, for literature was spared the attrition born of academicism. Literature—in whose view the human condition is inevitably a drama of conflict—has always been interested in man as a creature with some capacity, even if only potential, for independent personal volition: the one human capacity above all others that gives both interest and meaning to the literary records of conflicts between man and man, man and the world, or within man himself. It can hardly surprise us to find that the subject of will—*explicitly and literally*—has engaged the interest of authors as diverse as Flaubert, Butler, Goncharov, Tolstoy, Dostoyevsky, Ibsen, and even such moderns as Allen Tate and Lionel Trilling.

Having acknowledged my sympathy for those who preferred to abandon the matter of will, given its tedious, moralistic, and sterile expressions in the scholarship of the past, I should now like to consider the price—or, more precisely, the theoretical and practical consequences—of this abandonment. The problem may be briefly put in this manner: *without a clear and explicit conception of will as responsible mover, we tend to smuggle will into our psychological systems under other names—this contraband will being usually an irresponsible mover of our lives.* A corollary to this proposition is: *when particular aspects of our will-less systems are asked to become or include will, the existential or phenomenological relevance of these aspects is diminished.* Thus, when Freud shifted from will to libido, in the example mentioned earlier, he was forced to slight the phenomenological investigation of sexuality in favor of argument or polemics, insisting on the libido's distinction as prime mover. In his postscript to the case of Dora, he wrote: "I was further anxious to show that sexuality . . . provides the motive power for every single symptom, and for every manifestation of a symptom."[2] It could be said, I think, that every system, including my own, contains a polemic for its particular prime mover, such po-

---

[2] *Ibid.*, p. 137.

lemic being antithetical to the phenomenological illumination of the system's prime mover. In other words, when Freud insisted that sexuality be the will of his system, it was his and ultimately our understanding of the place of sexuality in existence that suffered from this double burden.

I shall do no more than list some of the categories that have been made to do the work of the will in various psychologies: unconscious, aggression, dependence, power, inferiority, sadomasochism, guilt, and, of course, anxiety. But, before I move to the matter of anxiety, I should like to say a word about the issue of psychological determinism itself, as it pertains to the will. Here I deal, not with prime movers, but with myriad small movers that appear to the imagination of the psychotherapist as chains of explanation the scrutiny of which may reveal to him the order he is intent on discovering in neurotic and psychotic disorder. A critical question here, or so it seems to me, is how motive may be distinguished from will. It would seem that, in psychology at least, when will was abandoned in our theories, motivation became an object of increasing concern. Motive and will have some superficial resemblance in that they both provoke movement or action. If I disparage my friend's achievements out of envy, envy is the motive of my disparagement. However, envy is not the same as will, even though my will to disparage may be incited by my motive of envy. In other words, a motive cannot be responsible for an action of will, even though it may provoke or prompt such action. This has been the usual distinction between will and motive. Obviously, a psychology of will would not preclude psychic determinism, even though it might deprive determinism of some of the ill-begotten prerogatives it has acquired in this century. It is when motive is used as cause that it begins to usurp the will's domain and at the same time defeat the phenomenological venture. If, out of envy, I will to disparage, I still have the option of willing not to disparage.

So far as I know, no such option occurs in disparagement whose cause is envy. The determinism relevant to these considerations seems more a professional tic, peculiar to psychotherapists, and might more accurately be called the compulsion or will toward causality that constructs, inventing in its own image, other wills called motives. If there is a motive provoking the will toward causality, it would not be causality itself, but rather the need for order or perhaps the intolerance of mystery. Such a will, when asked to explore the *what* of a situation, turns instead to the *why*. It is but another example of Yeats's "will trying to do the work of the imagination." The will toward causality, given its imaginative limitations, spawns prior wills, preceded by prior wills, and so on. Ideally, one hopes that principles may eventually arise out of the imaginative search of the situation itself, but here the principles arrive first, and any phenomena developed are at the mercy of these principles.

With these introductory remarks, I have tried to suggest the direction of my dissatisfaction with anxiety theory. To begin with, I am never entirely sure what the nature of the experience is that anxiety is meant to describe. It is unusually difficult to know whether anxiety signifies a particular shudder of being, common to us all, or whether anxiety is a general category, a blanket term meant to cover a range of painful states. Before the advent of modern psychology, it was one of many expressions we used to indicate distress; its meaning, according to *Webster's*, is "painful uneasiness of mind over an impending or anticipated ill." This meaning is, it seems to me, quite precise when compared to its present swollen and ambiguous condition whereby, depending on the whim of its user, it may indicate (or conceal) a host of distressing responses, with any number of subjective or objective shadings —emotional, cognitive, or physical. What we call "anxiety" today might in another time be more exactly rendered as "apprehension," "fear," "fright," "tremor," "uncertainty," "uneasiness," "dread," "restlessness," "worry," "shakiness," "trepidation," "desperation," "palpitations," "queasiness," "agitation," "anguish," "alienation," or "cowardice," according to which experience we wished to describe. It might be objected that theoretical speculation cannot, if only for the sake of brevity, afford such novelistic precision as it searches for hypothetical principles that will govern its theory. After all, we have many items of theory that are not to be confused with experience—ego, projection, regression, identification, and the like. But it must be answered that the abstract nature of these terms was clear from the beginning, whereas with "anxiety" it was never clear whether the term indicated a particular experience or a way of theorizing about a variety of experiences. As a result, what was at first an abstraction now passes itself off as experience itself, rather than a way of talking about experience. In our scientific age, it is always a danger that a psychological term may trespass its original scientific boundaries. Once the trespass becomes convention, experience itself is vulgarized, since theories about experience inevitably subvert experience, much as our experience corrects our theories.

Those psychological theories that have developed within the medical tradition have given a physical emphasis to anxiety so that the "painful uneasiness" of the older definition is now one of the body rather than of the mind. Even when no description of the experience is attempted, what is implied is a bodily response comparable to that of fright whose predominant manifestations—subjectively and objectively—are such physical disturbances as rapid heartbeat, tremors, dry mouth, overbreathing, sweating, muscular incoordination, insomnia, and so on. In this view, it is the bodily commotion that is primary, other aspects of our distress being derivative of this disturbance. The seeming advantage of a physical theory of anxiety is that the similarity of objective manifestations in babies and lower mammals allows a biological or evolutionary continuity to be asserted about all mammalian life when endangered. Partly because the subjectivity of lower animals cannot be inspected and partly because human danger need not be of the literal order of the jungle, a distinction is usually made in these theories between fear and anxiety. Whatever theoretical virtue this distinction may have, in actuality it is usually rather difficult, if not impossible, to separate objective from subjective danger. Needless to say, it is this bodily view of anxiety that has found common cause with the drug industry.

To pursue further the ambiguity of the experience of anxiety, let us consider briefly several modern definitions whose emphasis is not so physical. Kurt Goldstein describes anxiety as, in part, the subjective experience of the organism in a catastrophic condition.[3] Despite the fact that Goldstein's contributions have been in the general area of the medical sciences, it will be noted that his description makes no mention of objective bodily disturbance, but instead refers to subjective experience. Yet anxiety is for Goldstein clearly a categorical abstraction intended to cover a range of experience accompanying catastrophe. In an effort to be more particular about the human experience, Rollo May defines anxiety as "the apprehension cued off by a threat to some value which the individual holds essential to his existence as a personality."[4] The word "apprehension" has the virtue of having both psychic and physical implications. In contrast, Sullivan's descriptions are indeed abstract, suggesting some sort of unpleasant state brought on by the apprehension of disapproval in interpersonal relations.[5] Perhaps the most exhaustive de-

[3] Rollo May, *The Meaning of Anxiety* (New York: The Ronald Press Co., 1950), p. 49.
[4] *Ibid.*, p. 191.
[5] *Ibid.*, p. 148.

scription of the experience is contained in Karen Horney's definition of "basic anxiety," namely, "the feeling of being small, insignificant, helpless, deserted, endangered, in a world that is out to abuse, cheat, attack, humiliate, betray, envy."[6] This picture of helplessness in the face of a threatening world has a more hysterical, even paranoid, quality, in that the anxious person feels put upon and persecuted by the will of others but lacks any corresponding will to defend himself.

In summary, then, it seems clear that anxiety is a painful state invoked by threat to human integrity. But, in the theories we have considered, the experience of anxiety has been relatively neglected in favor of its causes and especially its consequences.

If I may return to an earlier proposition, the phenomenological thinness or ambiguity of the term "anxiety" as it appears in the theories I have just mentioned is largely the consequence of the burden laid on it to do the work of the will; that is, though unequal to the task, anxiety has been required to supply force, shape, meaning, and intention to the matter of psychological development and/or disability. Unlike the will, which pushes actively toward its goal, whether appropriate or inappropriate, anxiety is an ache that helplessly cries for relief. We are told by these theories that its painful urgency is so compelling as to overpower our discriminations, forcing us to settle for familiar and childish ways that serve us poorly in our life in the world. In passing, however, it should be remarked that the notion of settling for old ways is an unwitting attempt to smuggle the traditional will into the system. Be that as it may, the inevitability of pathological consequence associated with anxiety assists the cause of psychic determinism almost too well, failing to account for those times when, in spite of present or future pain, we choose a course that seems right rather than soothing.

[6] Karen Horney, *The Neurotic Personality of Our Time* (New York: W. W. Norton & Co., 1937), p. 92.

In order to contain this eventuality, some theories devise two anxieties, one normal and the other neurotic—the former liberating, the later constricting. In terms of experience, "normal" anxiety does not differ from neurotic anxiety and therefore is not to be confused with an ontological meaning that "anxiety" has carried for centuries, namely, solicitous or earnest desire. An example of this meaning would be "I am anxious to rejoin my friend." Although the addition of "normal anxiety" to a system would seem to allow anxiety more of the prerogatives of will, in effect it undercuts the original notion of anxiety as an insistent anguish compelling relief. Here a proposition could be made that, whenever a psychological category is asked to do the work of the will in psychopathology, sooner or later a normative version of that category must be added to the theory.

In order to consider further the issue of will and anxiety, I shall now confine myself to the theories and practice of Harry Stack Sullivan. According to him, the self is born of anxiety, or as he says, the self "comes into being as a dynamism to preserve the feeling of security."[7] Being an unpleasant feeling, anxiety requires relief. And the relief it finds is apt to be limiting to the development of the person. Whenever these limitations are overstepped, anxiety arises again and dissociates these new threats from awareness. Whatever existential content there may be to anxiety in his theories, it is evident that his is a most hypochondriacal view of development of the self. Unlike the traditional will, anxiety permits no choice, sees no ends, cannot discriminate between one course and another. In fact, since anxiety is always limiting, it would seem it insists on not only immediate but also on inferior relief. As such, the self is a tangle of makeshift adjustments, all hastily and mistakenly contrived for the sake of allaying anxiety. The system

[7] Harry Stack Sullivan, *Concepts of Modern Psychiatry* (Washington, D.C.: William Alanson White Foundation, 1947), p. 21.

has no room for accident, risk, surprise, mystery, or grace. In Sullivan's melancholy view, there seems no hope except through psychotherapy.

It may be interesting here to say something of how his theory shaped his practice. Since Sullivan was one of my teachers, I can be anecdotal about this issue. Some psychotherapists profess one theory, but in practice seem to pursue another. They may write about mankind as a jungle of destructive strife, in which survival is almost accidental, and yet in their office life be the most kind and considerate men. But, I would say of Sullivan, that he was one of the most painfully consistent human beings I have known: he not only wrote of anxiety as the center of his theories—he also practiced it. In this he resembled some of the more active Zen masters I have read about—men with devilish skill in inventing all manner of mental and physical devices for unsettling their pupils. In the interest of accuracy, I should say here that Sullivan was a mild man physically: he did not cudgel with sticks, he never raised his voice, and his harshest physical mannerism was a glance which never met my own. Believing psychotherapeutic ineptitude, as well as psychological disability in general, to stem from and to consist of our poor efforts to cope with anxiety, he thought that any psychotherapy or teaching worth its name must eventually provoke that anxiety, in the hope that within such ambience something more satisfactory might at long last occur. Our first meeting, which had taken several months to arrange and required the intervention of a mutual friend, was, to put it mildly, distressing. As I described the three patients I was treating at the time, he looked quite discouraged by the supervisory prospect. Two of my patients, he wearily explained, were wholly unsuitable for supervision and by inference, for psychotherapy, too. As I was beginning to wonder what presumption had possessed me to seek supervision with this eminent man, he grudgingly agreed to hear about my

37

third patient, although he made it quite clear he expected no good to come of it. This patient was a young man with severe ulcerative colitis, much of whose energy was spent, when he was not hospitalized, in both inviting and defeating the possessive intrusions of his divorced parents. For two hours, Sullivan sat in silence as I nervously tried to depict this young man's struggles, hoping all the while that my portrayal, while remaining faithful to my patient on the one hand, would be intriguing enough on the other to justify Sullivan's continuing to spend time with me in supervision. But he was too scrupulous, or too unimpressed, to indicate, through gesture or word, the tiniest interest in my account. Once or twice, when my desperation verged on sheer panic, I turned helplessly to him for advice, but he refused these overtures with a tired wave of the hand, as though my solicitations were too flagrant or too gross to deign a verbal refusal. When I finally ground to a limp and chaotic halt in my story and made ready to flee this unhappy occasion, Sullivan roused himself to offer what the Zen masters would call a *koan*. "I would suggest," he said, "that until our next appointment you try to imagine—mind you, not say, *imagine*—how your young man might respond if you were to ask him what he imagined his mother's reaction would be to his saying, 'Mother, since you insist you are so deeply attached to me, let us go to bed together and have it over with.'" If I may translate this rather involved imaginative exercise, Sullivan was suggesting that, out of my own anxiety, I was taking my patient's account of his parents' erotic attachment to him much too literally.

When I managed to drag myself to his study two weeks later for our second appointment, he immediately asked me if I had had any thoughts about our first session. I confessed I had not really been up to thought; in fact, my anguish had been so paralyzing that I had taken to my bed for most of the period. Deliberately I skipped the details of my anguish, the consuming self-disparagement that had led me to question even my choice of profession. His astonishing reply was, "Well, that's rather promising. I hadn't really expected so much." To this day I can still almost physically recall the relief and gratitude that came over me at having earned, in such an unexpected way, this man's approval through my suffering.

I trust I have conveyed in this vignette Sullivan's way of practicing what he preached. Unfortunately, what I have been forced to slight in this anecdote is his remarkable clinical shrewdness as well as his tactful, often compassionate, manner of dealing with disturbance such as mine. It should be noted that, according to his view, it was the anxiety over my patient that led me into gullibility; however, when Sullivan reinvoked that same anxiety, he provided me with the opportunity for new knowledge about myself and my work with the patient. In a way, this theory resembles a species of folk wisdom which occurs in several forms: anything really good comes hard, or nothing really good comes easy. At first, it would seem that Sullivan had reversed this belief, with the resultant conclusion that whatever comes hard is necessarily good. But such an assumption would be a serious underestimation: he was too knowing a psychotherapist and too convinced of the crippling power of anxiety to subscribe to such a reversal. Anxiety requires psychotherapeutic assistance, if the patient or student is not to return to old ways.

I should now like to re-examine the episode from the standpoint of will. Having already pressed the phenomenological question about anxiety as experience, I shall arbitrarily, and perhaps mistakenly, assume in what is to follow that anxiety in Sullivan's theories is a satisfactory rubric for the range of unhappiness which befell me. Somewhere in Sullivan's writings he has a footnote to the effect that he was one of those fortunate human beings without any anxiety to speak of. If this was so, and I have no reason to doubt it, our relationship—in this respect, at least—was somewhat uneven. True, I stood to gain more than he in this inequality, since he could not profit from old anxieties reinvoked, but at least he could be comforted by his trusting belief in his own unassailable acumen. To begin with the matter of my own will, I would have to postulate two forms that my will took, even as I made the long journey to my first appointment with him. On the one hand, there was the will to become a psychotherapist, which could be expressed as an enduring and wholehearted wish to become a capable member of the profession. This expression is more explicit than the fact that I pursued a goal or was pursued by it, without so baldly formulating this pursuit. Such will came and went, depending on discouragement, on my shifting estimation of what psychotherapy might be, my waverings as to the worldly ways in which best to find my professional career, and, of course, the doubts plaguing me from time to time as to whether "psychotherapist" described in any important way the man I wished to become. At any rate, it was this will that effected the intricate arrangements that culminated in my time with Sullivan. In referring to this will, I delete backslidings and hesitations and confusions that were to give way to a more self-conscious and stubborn determination to trudge through the course of psychoanalytic apprenticeship regardless of how my mind and body lagged in the process, regardless of the fatigue and boredom associated with this tiring and tiresome program. On the one hand, I wished to have supervisory time with such a renowned teacher in order to become a psychotherapist, whatever that was; on the other hand, I wished to impress him in order to become a favored pupil on my way to a diploma—and I knew what *that* was.

Sullivan's strategy or technique during our first meeting was characterized by his will not to respond. Regardless of intention, his deliberate indifference opposed my own will in two different ways. To the extent to which I gave myself wholeheartedly to my task, with all resources joined to my will to become a psychotherapist under his tutelage, there was a dialogic possibility open to us, whose rebuff no doubt led to the agonizing question of my suitability for the profession I had chosen. At a lower, more self-serving and self-seeking level, my determination to win his admiration was easily routed by his will not to respond. I could no more will to admire him, than I could will him to admire me. If I try to will my admiration of another, all I can grasp is the visage or posture of admiration: its actuality will elude me. If I try to will another to admire me, I shall self-consciously select only those gestures which are coercive of my end: regardless of my powers, he would have to be gullible indeed to be won by such manipulation. Willing what cannot be willed is by necessity an uneasy, even frantic, misdirection of the will: no cunning is required on the part of an adversary to bring such distress into frank and painful prominence. My guess is that, as every overture of mine was repudiated, my distress or anxiety grew, and, moreover, I was increasingly deprived of the few intellectual powers that were available to me, so that toward the end of our first appointment my will to impress Sullivan stood in harsh contrast with the uninspired and labored account to which I had been reduced. Even when he was later encouraged by the anxiety he had aroused in me, my relief was tempered by an awareness that, although he could will anxiety in me, I could not will anxiety in myself. Only the mannerisms of anxiety would be accessible to me, and these would not only fool no one but would defeat our joint pedagogical and therapeutic goal.

Out of my particular miseries with Sullivan, I wish now to define the relation between will and anxiety. In my understanding, the word anxiety is a broad term for human distress that contains a range of psychic and physical manifestations. With the exception of one additional phrase, anxiety in my usage does not differ essentially from *Webster's* definition, namely, a painful uneasiness of mind and body respecting an impending or anticipated ill. At any given moment, depending on which manifestations are most pressing, the experience of anxiety may be more exactly identified as uneasiness, trepidation, and the like (see page 33), without losing its tie to the parent category, anxiety. But, by whatever name it is called, *anxiety is that range of distress which attends willing what cannot be willed*. In other words, anxiety can be located in the ever-widening split between the will and the impossible object of the will. As the split widens, the bondage between the will and its object grows, so that one is compelled to pursue what seems to wither or altogether vanish in the face of such pursuit.

Before considering the implications of this definition, I should like to stress that my formulation is intended to be a phenomenological definition. As such, it would supplement rather than contradict other definitions of anxiety mentioned earlier, which are concerned, for the most part, with the causes and/or consequences of anxiety. Thus, in regard to Kurt Goldstein's definition, mine would explore the nature of "the subjective experience," as well as something of the "catastrophic condition" into which the "organism" falls in anxiety. In regard to Rollo May's definition, my definition does not attempt to contend with the "threat" to values which causes anxiety, but rather with the experience itself which follows such a threat. My purpose is to extend phenomenologically what Rollo May calls "apprehension."

If my life in the world is threatened by loss, betrayal, failure, disapproval, or injury, I may respond in various ways depending on who and where I am in my world and on the exact nature and relevance of the threat endangering me. Melancholy, grief, despair, remorse, and enlightenment are but a few of the possibilities open to me, even when the threat is to values I deem essential to my existence. But anxiety, I would emphasize, is not my lot until I resort to my will to counter such threat and now will what cannot be willed. The severity of my impairment will vary according to the degree to which the will, in bondage to its object, is isolated from such faculties as reason, imagination, and the like, and the degree to which the object being willed recedes and diminishes in the rush of will. It is important to stress that the disability is principally one of will, because a serious deficiency of anxiety theory has been the inability of anxiety itself to account for the human mishaps it would explain. We need no special clinical background to remind ourselves of those who are privately and visibly anxious without any particular disorder in their lives as a result of anxiety. This must mean that, in the midst of anxiety, crucial faculties are still available. On the other hand, we should be equally familiar with those who neither have nor have had any great anxiety in their lives, yet their difficulties are enormous. Here, it is simply not enough for anxiety theory to invoke the "little-man-who-wasn't-there" psychologism, asserting that anxiety could be there if it weren't so immediately assuaged by defensive and inferior stratagems. Since this inference cannot be argued, demonstrated, nor—more important—confirmed in the experience of the placid ones, belief in it must remain an article of faith in the dogma of anxiety theory. It is but another instance of making anxiety do the work of the will, said work unfortunately being shoddy and unconscious. It is worth remarking on, however, that when either the anxious ones or the placid ones are asked to investigate the circumstances surrounding their anxiety or placidity, the result may be salutary even though it may not prove the theory. Salutary, because in either case the will has been offered a suitable endeavor for its efforts which hopefully will help return the world which has been lost or acquire a world which never was.

It follows that to characterize the nature of my encounter with Sullivan as mere anxiety would do it phenomenological injustice. At the same time, to abstract anxiety for theoretical purposes as the psychological mover toward either constriction or enlightenment would be equally fallacious. Anxiety may be an ache which cries for relief, but whether or what relief will occur cannot be a result of anxiety's decision. Unlike the will, anxiety must be considered morally (or psychologically) *inert*, which is to say that, whether good or evil follows, anxiety will depend on forces other than anxiety. My will to become a psychotherapist, though seriously shaken, allowed me to contend with a more meretricious need to impress Sullivan. I doubt very much that the anxiety which accompanied my willing what could not be willed—given his will not to respond—was in itself generative of insight about myself or my patient. Recognizing my own gullibility in work with my patient was, as far as I can see, a response to Sullivan's clinical shrewdness—not because of, but *in spite of, anxiety*. Conceivably, I might have chosen another way through which, indicting the man as cruel, arrogant, and a poor teacher, I did not return. Such a conclusion could have been willed only by blinding myself to my discriminations of this remarkable man. Had that been my way, I should no doubt have told myself and a few close friends that I was forced to discontinue because of the anxiety he provoked in me.

As has already been suggested, the more stubborn the will's pursuit of its intractable goal, the sooner it will be separated from those faculties that might allow its bondage to be objectified, diverted, or dispelled. In isolation from such powers as intellect and imagination, the will can only will, reflection about its own adversities being beyond its capacity. The failure of meaning, which is said to be characteristic of anxiety, stems from the deprivation of resources and the withering of the will's goal in the face of the will's demands. Because of this failure, the anxious person may eventually no longer be able to say what he is anxious about. However, his failure should not be attributed, as is the habit, to the fact that the cause of his anxiety has been repressed, but rather to the fact that those rational powers that might assist the will have fallen away and will not return until, for one reason or another, there is an end to willing what cannot be willed. This same failure in self-reflection has often been used to distinguish anxiety from fear whose cause, or so it is assumed, is actual and exterior. According to this view, the danger in anxiety is "inner" and unknown, while the danger provoking fear is "outer" and known. Even if we try to preserve a legitimate distinction between anxiety and fear, although I believe psychology has misused this distinction, it can readily be seen that both experiences have their inner and outer dimensions. So far as the present definition is concerned, fear does not merge into anxiety until willing what cannot be willed takes over. If I am summoned to an interview with a superior who, I am warned, will be sharply critical of my performance, my troubled anticipation of this event will contain, in addition to my willing, a mingling of subjective and objective considerations, but I doubt that it is either useful or possible to disentangle that portion of my apprehension which may be inner anxiety and that portion which may be outer fear.

A burst of thunder in a darkening sky can frighten me with the possibility that the plane in which my family is flying home will be caught in the same impending storm. Again, the inner and outer features of my unhappy state seem less critical than the degree to which I now fall into willing what cannot be willed: clear skies, gifted pilot, indestructible plane. Untempered by imagination and reason, not to mention information from the weather bureau and airport, my isolated will *wills*—that is, it demands its object absolutely, however futile

4 5

that demand may be. And, with each new crack of thunder, I shall no doubt swing from the willed certainty of safety to the certainty of disaster, so that now the storm battering that fragile plane is violent, and the pilot hopelessly inept. Both obsessive extremes, with their attendant anxiety, are products of my isolated will. Should I, still in the mood of disaster, muse about how to bury my family and take up my life alone, it must be construed that my musings are born of that same isolated will, rather than a hostile, if unacceptable, instinct for their destruction. Were I to assume that such a motive supported my will in its authorship of these melancholy reveries, my disorder would still lie in willing what cannot be willed—namely, the storm's destruction of plane and family. Moreover, for the sake of completeness, I should have to assume a more considerate motive to account for my insistence on their safety.

If only because of their extreme and uncommon character, the conventional illustrations of fear to be found in the usual anxiety theory tend to reveal the effort to rid the problem of contamination by subjectivity: the armed burglar in the night, the rabid bat in the bedroom, the car careening toward us on the wrong side of the road. Yet even these examples, so weighted on the objective side, would seem to fail in their purpose. Presumably, immediate overpowering fright will give way to anxiety at the point that we retrospectively resort to willing what cannot be willed. But even that very first fright, so far as we can penetrate the experience, carries no lesson in the epistemology of danger from without. Little reflection is required to realize that it, too, must mingle both inner and outer aspects. Clearly, it is as hard to construct an anxiety that is only inner, as it is to imagine a fear that is only outer.

In the disability of will that we have been considering, anxiety is not the only experience. As the will is increasingly stripped of supporting faculties, and as what is being willed recedes further from the will's impositions, the will itself comes to be experienced as impotent thrust. It is the very powerlessness of the power pressing toward its refractory goal that accounts for the helplessness and uncertainty that most writers believe to be essential characteristics of anxiety. As discernment fails, what can most painfully be discerned are those bodily manifestations of distress which have occupied the medical approach to the subject of anxiety. Thus, the split between the will and its object, if extended in time and severity, enforces finally another split between mind and body in which our world, already diminished by the bondage described, shrinks still further to that cramped cell where all we can do is suffer and observe those painful commotions of our flesh. And, these bodily discomforts again oppose, even as they invite, the activities of our isolated will. This is the arena, peculiarly modern, which can loosely be described as fear of fear or anxiety about anxiety. More accurately, it is the shrunken state in which, as actor and audience of our body's disabilities, we will not to have anxiety, such willing bringing more anxiety in its wake. This impasse may well be the existential source for the biological or medical views of the problem of anxiety.

This has been called the "Age of Anxiety." Considering the attention given the subject by psychology, theology, literature, and the pharmaceutical industry, not to mention the testimony from our own lives, we could fairly well conclude that there is more anxiety today, and, moreover, that there is definitely more anxiety about anxiety now than there has been in previous epochs of history. Nevertheless, I would hesitate to characterize this as an "Age of Anxiety," just as I would be loath to call this an "Age of Affluence, "Coronary Disease," "Mental Health," "Dieting," "Conformity," or "Sexual Freedom," my reason being that none of these labels, whatever fact or truth they may involve, goes to the heart of the matter. Much as I dislike this game of labels, my preference, which could be anticipated, would be to call this the "Age of the Disordered Will." It takes only a glance to see a few of the myriad varieties of willing what cannot be willed that enslave us: we will to sleep, will to read fast, will to have simultaneous orgasm, will to be creative and spontaneous, will to enjoy our old age, and, most urgently, will to will. If anxiety is more prominent in our time, such anxiety is the product of our particular modern disability of the will. To this disability, rather than to anxiety, I would attribute the every-increasing dependence on drugs affecting all levels of our society. While drugs do offer relief from anxiety, their more important task is to offer the illusion of healing the split between the will and its refractory object. The resulting feeling of wholeness may not be a responsible one, but at least within that wholeness—no matter how willful the drugged state may appear to an outsider—there seems to be, briefly and subjectively, a responsible and vigorous will. This is the reason, I believe, that the addictive possibilities of our age are so enormous.

At the same time that our lives are occupied by deliberate efforts of will, toward both appropriate and inappropriate ends, with or without drugs we suffer a mounting hunger for a sovereign and irreducible will, so wedded to our reason, our emotions, our imagination, our intentions, and our bodies that, only after a given enterprise has come to an end, can we retrospectively infer that will was present at all. In other words, within such totality, will, being unconscious, would not be a matter of experience, even though we might later try to portray the essence of the enterprise as one in which we wished with our whole heart or willed with all our being. The predominant experience within this realm of will would be one of freedom, as opposed to the bondage of the isolated will. The goal of will within this realm would be one of direction rather than of a specific object or achievement, although naturally the course of this will would be dotted inconspicuously by such concrete items. Never a permanent state and always limited in duration, it would give way over and over again to the more self-conscious will with which we are necessarily more familiar. Needless to say, utilitarian opportunities for this more self-conscious will are vast in this technological age; in fact, it could be said that our technology could not have been accomplished without it. To move my hand, add a column of figures, even earn a psychoanalytic diploma are all discrete and feasible objects for this will. However, there is no activity I could mention, however trivial, which, in the service of the joined realm of will, would not lose its utilitarian countenance and become part of the flow in a particular direction. I may say I went to the library to look at a book that I thought might be interesting. By all standards, this is an ordinary statement about an ordinary errand, requiring no comment except that the errand and the statement about it are singularly unmuscular in nature and point merely in the direction of possible interest. If I am asked, on my return from the library, for the physical details of my trip, I shall probably—and fortunately—not remember them. However, when my utilitarian will engineers this errand, something ordinary is now splintered into many things arduous. *Book* now becomes the principal object of this expedition, but of course there are subsidiary objects, too: I must pick the proper time, choose the right route, park on a crowded street, deal with a difficult librarian, and so on. Once the book is found, *reading the book* can splinter into similar tedious efforts of will, all open to memory, should someone be foolish enough to inquire. Though tedious and arduous, these actions are still feasible and, in their difficulty, will not compare with the anxiety that arises when this same utilitarian will is asked to will what it cannot will.

Consideration of the historical origins of our present situation lies outside my purpose and competence. I would, however, ask this question: could it be that the disordered will, with its paradoxical privilege for technology and all manner of scientific fact, and the hunger from which we suffer for another will, are the consequence of the death of God proclaimed by Nietzsche in the last century? If so, few of us, I suspect, believers and nonbelievers alike, have been spared. Depending on which side of Nietzsche's divide we stand historically, the other side is almost unimaginable. For this reason, the contemporary issue is not of the order proposed by Kirillov in Dostoyevsky's *The Possessed:* "To recognize that there is no God and not to recognize at the same instant that one is God oneself is an absurdity, else one would certainly kill oneself." Kirillov's choice, springing from its apparent logical necessity, has the terrified, yet abstract, quality of one who, while still on the other side of the divide, has glimpsed the loss, but that loss has not yet penetrated and shaped his life in all those subtle and pedestrian ways that make Nietzsche's proclamation for most of us merely another old-fashioned theological generalization. With the disappearance of the divine Will from our lives, we have come to hunger not for His Will—neither in the sense of living in His Will nor usurping His Will for ourselves—but rather for our own sovereign will, which is our modern way, this side the omnipotence of suicide or madness. And all exhortations notwithstanding, this will we cannot will.

3

I'M SORRY, DEAR

> And the eyes of them both were opened, and they knew that they were naked; and they sewed fig leaves together, and made themselves aprons.
>
> —GENESIS

> Lust is more abstract than logic; it seeks (hope triumphing over experience) for some purely sexual, hence purely imaginary, conjunction of an impossible maleness with an impossible femaleness.
>
> —C. S. LEWIS[1]

The modern dialogue that furnishes me my title is practiced throughout the Western world. As a theme with only a limited number of variations, it cannot sustain much repetition: familiarity breeds silence; although never really abandoned, the script quickly becomes implicit. When reduced to a dumb show—or perhaps no more than a monosyllabic token—it still remains faithful to its pathetic premise. However, for the purposes of introduction, I shall try to represent its essence in a wholly explicit manner. The man speaks first.

"Did you?"

"Did *you?* You *did,* didn't you?"

"Yes, I'm afraid I—Oh, I'm sorry! I *am* sorry. I know how it makes you feel."

"Oh, don't worry about it. I'm sure I'll quiet down after a while."

[1] C. S. Lewis, *The Allegory of Love* (New York: Oxford University Press, 1958), p. 196.

"I'm *so* sorry, dearest. Let me help you."

"I'd rather you didn't."

"But, I . . ."

"What good is it when you're just—when you don't really want to? You know perfectly well, if you don't *really* want to, it doesn't work."

"But I *do really* want to! I *want* to! Believe me. It *will* work, you'll see. Only let me!"

"Please, couldn't we just forget it? For now the thing is done, finished. Besides, it's not really that important. My tension always wears off eventually. And anyhow—maybe next time it'll be different."

"Oh, it *will*, I *know* it will. Next time I won't be so tired or so eager. I'll make sure of that. Next time it's going to be *fine!* . . . But about tonight—I'm sorry, dear."

Unhappily, no end to talking and trying for our pathetic lovers. To deaden self-consciousness, they may turn to alcohol or sedatives, seeking the animal indifference that is unencumbered with hesitations, reservations, and grievances—in short, all those human tangles that create the sexual abyss they will themselves to bridge. To delay his moment, to quicken hers, they may try to assist the chemicals by thinking of other matters—football games and cocktail parties—in order finally to arrive at that mutual consummation that, hopefully, will prove their sufficiency unto each other, if not their love. All the strategies and prescriptions of sexology that have often failed them in the past are not cast aside, but stubbornly returned to, if only because in such an impasse there is nothing else. Instead of alcohol or drugs or irrelevant reveries they may—in solitude or mutuality—resort to sex itself as their sedative, intending in the first try to spend their energies just enough to dull self-consciousness and thicken passion to the "spontaneity" necessary for their second and final attempt.

Although normally truthful people, our lovers are continually tempted by deception and simulation: he may try to conceal his moment, she to simulate hers—as they stalk their equalitarian ideal. It can happen that they will achieve simultaneity by means of one or several or none of these devices. But their success—in the midst of their congratulations—will be as dispiriting as their failures. For one thing, the joy the lovers sought in this manner will be either absent or too fictitious to be believed. Furthermore, once the moment has subsided they must reckon with the extraordinary efforts that brought it about—efforts that appear too extraordinary for ordinary day-to-day existence. Thus does it happen that success may bring as much as, or more, pathos than failure. And, always lying between them will be the premise borrowed from romanticism: if they *really* loved each other, it would work. Small wonder, then, as self-pity and bitterness accumulate, that their musings—if not their actions—turn to adultery: a heightened situation that promises freedom from the impingements of ordinary sexual life. Or, pushed gradually past heightening, past hope, they may even come to abstinence, which can seem—with some irony—the least dishonorable course.

My conviction is that over the last fifty years sex has, for the most part, lost its viability as a human experience. I do not mean that there is any danger it will cease to be practiced—that it will be put aside like other Victorian bric-a-brac. The hunger will remain, perhaps even increase, and human beings will continue to couple with as much fervor as they can provoke, while the human possibilities of sex will grow ever more elusive. Such couplings will be poultices after the fact: they will further extend the degradation of sex that has resulted from its ever-increasing bondage to the modern will. To those first pioneers at the turn of the century—sexologists, psychoanalysts, political champions of woman's suffrage—

53

"sexual emancipation" seemed a stirring and optimistic cause. Who could have imagined then, as the battle was just beginning, how ironic victory would be: sex was emancipated, true, but emancipated from all of life—except the will—and subsequently exalted as the measure of existence.

At this point I think it only fair that I commit myself, even if briefly, on how sex was, is, or could be a viable human experience. My view is not that of St. Augustine—that man, by reason of the Fall, is necessarily subject to the lust of concupiscence. Nor can I subscribe, at the other extreme, to the position of the Church of England, as reported at the Lambeth Conference in 1958: "The new freedom of sexuality in our time is . . . a gate to a new depth and joy in personal relationship between husband and wife."[2] Of the erotic life, Martin Buber has remarked that in no other realm are dialogue and monologue so mingled and opposed. I would agree that any attempt to offer a normative description would have to include precisely such mingling and opposition. Even if we place it optimally within an ongoing domestic world of affection, in which sex bears some relation, however slight, to procreation, our task is still the difficult one of maintaining that sex is both utterly important and utterly trivial. Sex may be a hallowing and renewing experience, but more often it will be distracting, coercive, playful, frivolous, discouraging, dutiful, and even boring. On the one hand, it tempts man to omnipotence, while on the other, it roughly reminds him of his mortality. Over and over again it mocks rationality, only to be mocked, in turn, at the very instant it insists its domain is solely within the senses. Though it promises the suspension of time, no other event so sharply advises us of the oppressiveness of time. Sex offers itself as an alternative world, but when the act is over and the immodesty of this offering is exposed,

[2] Dorothea Krook, *Three Traditions of Moral Thought* (Cambridge: Cambridge University Press, 1959), p. 336.

it is the sheer worldliness of the world we briefly relinquished and must now re-enter that has to be confronted anew. Residing no longer in the same room that first enclosed us, we now lie in another room with another topography—a room whose surfaces, textures, corners, and knobs have an otherness as absolute and formidable as the duties and promises that nag us with their temporal claims. What began as relief from worldly concern, ends by returning us to the world with a metaphysical, if unsettling, clarity.

Though sex often seems to be morality's adversary, it more often brings sharply in its wake moral discriminations that previously had not been possible. Because the pleasure of sex is always vulnerable to a split into *pleasuring* and *being pleasured,* the nature of pleasure itself, as well as the relation between pleasure and power, are called into question. If pleasuring is the overpowering concern, intimations of the actual and immediate experience of slavery or peonage will appear. On the other hand, if being pleasured is the most compelling, tyranny and oppression will invade experience with some urgency. And, finally, should the lovers will equality between these two concerns in their effort to heal the split, they will personally suffer the problematic character of democratic forms. To some extent, our political past influences our sexual negotiations, but in equal measure sexual pleasure itself is a source of political practice and theory.

The list of oppositions and minglings could easily be extended, but such an extension would not change the fact that human sex inevitably partakes of human experience, for better or for worse, and through its claim on the body simultaneously asserts its particular difference, for better or for worse.

Its particular difference from everything else in this life lies in the possibility which sex offers man for regaining *his own* body through knowing the body of his loved one. Should he fail that *knowing* and *being known,* should he lapse

55

into all those ways of *knowing about* which he has proudly learned to confuse with knowing—both bodies will again escape him. Increasingly, as D. H. Lawrence understood, man has become separated from his body, which he yearns to inhabit, such yearning understandably bringing sentimental and scientific prescriptions for the reunion eluding him. Yet, it is through the brief reconciliation with his own and his loved one's body that he can now grasp—and endure—the bodily estrangement which has always been his lot, without succumbing to the blandishments that would betray the realities of both sides of this duality.

In order to develop more concretely my conviction that sex for the most part has lost its viability as a human experience, I wish to consider the Sex Research Project, directed by Dr. William H. Masters at the Washington University School of Medicine. Through the use of women volunteers, Dr. Masters is endeavoring "to separate a few basic anatomic and physiologic truths" about "the human female's response" to what he calls "effective sexual stimulation." The subject, he believes, has been hopelessly beclouded by "literary fiction and fantasy," "pseudoscientific essays and pronouncements," and "an unbelievable hodgepodge of conjecture and falsehood." His debt to Kinsey is clear, though qualified. He acknowledges his "complete awe" for Kinsey's "time-consuming efforts," which have made his own research not only "plausible, but possible." On the other hand, he finds that the work of his predecessors, including Kinsey, has unfortunately been "the result of individual introspection, expressed personal opinion, or of limited clinical observation"—rather than "a basic science approach to the sexual response cycle."[3] Therefore, he has done what was indeed inevitable: he has moved the whole investigation into the laboratory.

[3] William H. Masters, "The Sexual Response Cycle of the Human Female," *West. J. Surg., Obst. & Gynec.*, 68 (Jan.–Feb. 1960), p. 57.

I should make clear that Dr. Masters' project itself interests me far more than his exact findings. This project strikes me as one of those occasional yet remarkable enterprises that quite transcends, despite its creator's intentions, its original and modest scientific boundaries, so that it becomes a vivid allegory of our present dilemma, containing its own image of man—at the same time that it charts a New Jerusalem for our future. Such an enterprise, when constitutive, is apt to be more relevant and revealing than deliberate art. Because no actual artist is involved, it is not particularly rewarding to ask how this matter acquires its revelatory, even poetic, power. Often its director merely pursues the prevailing inclination in his field. Yet the pursuit is so single-minded, so fanatical and literal, that part of the power of the enterprise as constitutive symbol must be credited to the director's unflagging lack of imagination and his passionate naïveté, which stay undeterred by all the proprieties, traditions, and accumulated wisdom that would only complicate his course.

I shall not linger over the anatomical and physiological detail in Dr. Masters' reports, except to say it concerns the changes observed on the various parts of the bodies of his volunteers as they approach, accomplish, and depart from sexual climax. Of all the mechanical, electrical, and electronic devices at his command in this research, it is movie-making which seems to give Dr. Masters the clearest edge over the subjective distortions of his predecessors.

Since the integrity of human observation of specific detail varies significantly, regardless of the observer's training or good intent, colored motion-picture photography has been used to record in absolute detail all phases of the human sexual response cycle. The movie is a silent one. Wisely, I think, the director has omitted a sound track, for the tiny events of the flesh he wishes to depict are not audible. Moreover, had there been sound equipment, all one would have heard would have been those adventitious rustlings of any well-equipped laboratory, and perhaps the quickened breathing and gasping of the subjects.

The movie opens quite abruptly with a middle-distance shot of a naked woman, standing, her head and lower legs deliberately outside the movie-frame. One arm hangs at her side, the other is stretched toward her genitals in an Eve-like posture, except that it is immediately apparent she is caressing, rather than covering, her parts. More in the service of decorum than science, there are no close-ups of her hand. This opening scene of a faceless woman silently playing with herself against a neutral antiseptic laboratory background quickly sets the tone for what is to follow. The naked, yet faceless, body informs us this is a "human female" we are observing. The other bodies that will subsequently appear in the film will also be faceless; the viewer may momentarily wonder, as cuts are made from one body to another, if it is the same body he is looking at, until he becomes used to distinguishing one body from another by differences in shape of breasts, distribution of pubic hair, and the like. At no time do any scientists or technicians appear; they may be presumed to be standing fully clothed behind the camera. In any large dramatic sense, the arm manipulating the body's private parts furnishes the only real movement and cinematically asserts, even when not in view, that it will continue to fondle during the photographing of more microscopic and glandular events. Since what is to follow will focus on relatively small and minute areas of flesh that ordinarily would not be cinematic, the first shot of the moving hand heightens the dramatic effect of the oozings, engorgements, and contractions this flesh will undergo as climax approaches.

Following this middle-distance shot that is extended a bit in time to give the illusion of mounting excitement, the camera moves in on the skin of the abdomen and back, so that the film can record the first fine rash beginning to appear over the lower body.

Through the use of cuts, several bodies exhibit their rashes until the phenomenon is safely established. Now the camera moves to the breasts to portray distention, venous engorgement, and changes in the nipples. As these changes are repeated on a number of breasts, we must remind ourselves that the initial arm or arms are continuing their work, although it is obvious that views of such action must be suspended from time to time to allow for certain close-ups. Up to this point, all that occurs in the movie could take place on that lonely, upright body that appeared in the opening scene. Now, quite suddenly and without preparation, that body is no longer upright but supine, and the scene is a brilliantly lit close-up of the opening of the vagina. At this point, something of an operating-room atmosphere intrudes, largely because a speculum spreads the lips of the vagina apart to permit an unobstructed view of all that will occur during orgasm.

It is obvious from this portion of the movie that the source of vaginal lubrication is of special interest to the project, as evidenced by a series of ingenious shots of the wall of the vagina showing the formation of individual drops of secretion. The movie then proceeds with a rush to the point that has been imminent since the beginning—namely, orgasm—objective orgasm, displayed visually in the contractions around, and the dilations within, the vagina. The film ends, as might be anticipated, with a succession of photographs of other bodies undergoing similar spasms. With some shrewdness, the director has withstood the tempting aesthetic impulse to conclude his movie with a final shot of the upright naked body with both arms now hanging limply down.

This movie is often referred to in Dr. Masters' writings and, I am told, has been exhibited at a number of scientific institutes throughout the country. So fond is he of this medium that there seem to be occasions when his scientific prose seeks, however incompletely, to emulate, not only the objectivity, but the aesthetic brilliance of his movie sequences:

If the bright pink of the excitement phase changes to a brilliant primiparous scarlet-red, or the multiparous burgundy color, a satisfactory plateau phase has been achieved.[4]

There is even a point at which the movie medium itself becomes the inventor: like the accidental solution or the contaminated culture, which have heroic roles in older scientific romances, movie-making allows Dr. Masters to uncover "the vascular flush reaction to effective sexual stimulation" that had not been previously described in the scientific literature:

With the aid of artificially increased skin surface temperature, such as that necessary for successful motion-picture photography, the wide distribution of this flush becomes quite apparent. . . . With orgasm imminent, this measle-like rash has been observed to spread over the anterior-lateral borders of the thighs, the buttocks, and the whole body.[5]

Probably it was this discovery of the "measle-like rash" that inspired a more Pavlovian venture which, if read slowly, will be seen to have quite eerie dimensions:

One observed subject, undergoing electroencephalographic evaluation, had been trained for four months to attain orgasm without producing concomitant muscle tension in order to provide significance for her tracing pattern. Yet, this patient repeatedly showed a marked flush phenomenon over the entire body during plateau and orgasm, and during resolution was completely covered with a filmy, fine perspiration.[6]

If movie-making is his main laboratory device, "automanipulative techniques" constitute his "fundamental investigative approach" to "the sexual response cycle of the human female." His frankness here is to be commended, particularly since some scientists might feel that such automanipulation

[4] *Ibid.,* p. 63.
[5] *Ibid.,* p. 61.
[6] *Ibid.,* p. 61.

was inadequate to the verisimilitude necessary for laboratory demonstration. Dr. Masters himself does not discuss the issue, but his obvious preference for this approach over coitus does not appear to be ascribable to decorum. To some degree, I imagine, it was the laboratory procedures and devices—particularly motion-picture photography—which determined the approach, automanipulation being clearly more accessible to scientific inspection than coition. But, more important, there is evidence that Dr. Masters regards automanipulation to be a more reliable[7]—that is, a more predictable—technique than "heterosexual activity" in the pursuit of "the more intense, well-developed, orgasmic response" cycle.

This type of total pelvic reaction is particularly true for an orgasmic phase elicited by manual manipulation, but it also occurs, although less frequently, with coition.[8]

Yet even this approach, so admirably suited to laboratory research, must share part of the blame for Dr. Masters' in-

[7] In a later investigation of contraceptive devices, Dr. Masters is led to develop a research technique of "artificial coitus." (See William H. Masters and Virginia E. Johnson, "Intravaginal Contraceptive Study," *West. J. Surg., Obst. & Gynec.*, 70 [July–Aug. 1962], particularly pp. 202–203). Since it is not described in any detail, we cannot know whether the old limerick was its inspiration. (The one that goes, "There was a young man from Racine, Who invented a f——— machine," ending with "And was terribly easy to clean.") However, it does seem to involve an "artificial penis," whose principal virtue is that it "affords direct observation of the vaginal barrel during the entire female sexual response cycle." Its disadvantage, admittedly surmountable, lies in the fact that his volunteers did not immediately take to the method. "The technique of artificial coitus necessitates conditioning of these individuals to assure definitive research results. In every instance, all thirty members of the subject population . . . underwent three separate sessions to establish familiarity with, and effective response to, the artificial coital technique." Once again, the problem of verisimilitude is presented: how much threat of impregnation can this machine pose?

[8] William H. Masters and Virginia E. Johnson, "The Artificial Vagina: Anatomic, Physiologic, Psychosexual Function," *West. J. Surg., Obst. & Gynec.*, 69 (May–June 1961), p. 202.

ability to measure the "clitoral body" during sexual excitement.

The attempts to measure increases in clitoral size objectively have
been generally unsatisfactory due to the marked variation in size
and positioning of the normal clitoral body, and the multiplicity
of automanipulative techniques employed by the various subjects
under observation.[9]

Little is told us about the volunteers in this research. Apparently the project began with prostitutes. But when objections were made that such a profession might not yield the
best "normal" sample, subjects were chosen among medical
students and medical students' wives who volunteered and
were paid a modest fee for their activities. Naturally no studies
could be made on those who, for whatever reason, would not
volunteer. And, presumably quickly eliminated were those
young women who offered themselves out of their enthusiastic
wish to contribute to science, only to discover they could not
sustain their sexual excitement in the setting of the laboratory,
with the paraphernalia, the cameras, the technicians, and the
bright lights. Even more quickly eliminated were those women
who on initial interview were not sure whether or not they
had climax: "Our rule of thumb is if they're not sure about it,
they probably haven't had it."

Other circumstances surrounding the study can only be
guessed at. Like much scientific research, this particular
project must have been an orderly affair. It can be assumed
that the investigators did not wait on the whim of their volunteers; that is, they were not subject to call day or night whenever the volunteer felt in the mood. No, the women were
given regular appointments during the working day when the
entire research crew was available. Doubtless, too, the direc-
tors of the project considered it scientifically unseemly to
encourage sexual titillation in their volunteers—certainly out

[9] Masters, *op. cit.*, p. 62.

of the question would have been anything resembling a physical overture. Should suggestive reading matter be required by the research—as it indeed occasionally was—it would have to be offered the volunteers in a spirit of detachment; not even the hint of a smirk could be allowed to disrupt the sobriety of the occasion. On the whole, the erotic basis would have to be provided by the scientific situation itself, in addition to the actual manipulation: that is, the prospect of arriving at the laboratory at 10:00 A.M., disrobing, stretching out on the table, and going to work in a somewhat businesslike manner while being measured and photographed, would have to provide its own peculiar excitement. (Thank you, Miss Brown, see you same time next week. Stop at the cashier's for your fee.) So, back to one's ordinary existence.

If these speculations have any truth, what can be said about the qualities that the ideal subject for such experiments would have? In a general way, her sexuality would have to be autonomous, separate from, and unaffected by, her ordinary world. "World" here would have to include, not only affection, but all those exigencies of human existence which tend to shape our erotic possibilities. Objectively, her sexuality would be mechanically accessible or "on call"—under circumstances which would be, if not intimidating, at least distracting to most bodies. Hers would have to be indifferent to the entire range of experiences, pleasant and unpleasant, whose claim is not only not salacious but makes us forget there is such a thing as sexuality. Her lust would lie to hand, ready to be invoked and consummated, in sickness or in health, in coitus or "auto-manipulation," in homosexuality or heterosexuality, in exasperation or calm, hesitancy or certainty, playfulness or despair. (This would be the other side of that older, though not unrelated, romanticism which just as willfully insisted on soft lights, Brahms, incense, and poetical talk.) In other words,

63

her sexuality would be wholly subject to her will: whenever she determined—or the project determined—that she should reach a climax, she would willingly begin those gestures that would lead to one. To use the modern idiom, all that would be unavailable to her sexological dexterity would be frigidity. Or, to speak more clearly, all that would be unavailable to her would be a real response to the laboratory situation. Insofar as her sexuality was under her will's dominion, she would resemble those odd creatures on the old television quiz programs—also ideal subjects in their own way —who were led from boarding houses to stand in a hot sound-proof isolation booth, and when the fateful question was delivered from the vault, answered correctly and without a tremor how many words there were in *Moby Dick*—answered correctly in a loud clear voice under circumstances in which most of us could not even mumble our name. The popularity of these programs (at least until skulduggery was revealed) suggests the audience looked with envy and/or admiration at this caricature of knowledge—a knowledge equally responsive to its owner's will, regardless of contingency or trapping.

A truly constitutive symbol should embody both an accurate rendering of contemporary life and a clear indication of what that life should be. Taking, for the moment, only the ideal contained in my description of the volunteer in these experiments, I would say that she is a latterday Queen of Courtly Love, a veritable Queen Guinevere. For most modern men and women, who grow ever more discouraged by their bodies' stubborn refusal to obey their owners' will, this Lady of the Laboratory has long been the woman of their dreams: men long to channel or claim this creature's prompt and unspecific response for their own specific overtures, while women dream of rivaling her capacity to serve her body's need whenever she so wills.

And what of those self-effacing scientists behind the camera who conceived and guided this research? Do they too reflect

who we are and who we would become? We know as little
about this research team as we know about the volunteers.
How the scientific boundaries were staked out and protected
against trespass is not described in the reports. Once again, we
can only surmise, but that there was difficulty is suggested by
a remark Dr. Masters made in one of his lectures—namely,
that he preferred to have a woman scientist alongside him in
these investigations because she helped to make him or keep
him more "objective." I assume he meant that having an actual
woman present, fully clad in the white coat of science, reminded him, not only of the point of the matter at hand, but
of the more hazardous life to be lived with women outside the
laboratory—of the difference between the ideal and the actual.
It would be a ticklish problem how to maintain the proper
detachment to protect the scientists without at the same time
inhibiting the volunteers. Here, the equipment and rituals of
research would help. And, very possibly, there would be a
deliberate effort to eliminate even the ordinary frivolity that
sometimes overcomes a surgical team in the midst of the most
delicate operation, because frivolity in this sort of research
might be only a way-station en route to the lubricious. Any
falling-away into the most ordinary locker-room talk, in or
out of the laboratory, would have to be regarded as a danger
signal. I imagine each scientist, with all the resolution at his
command, would remind himself continually that it was just
an ordinary day's work in the laboratory, no different from
the work next door with the diabetic rats. At the end of the
day, when his wife asked, "How were things at the lab
today?" he would reply, "Oh nothing, just the same old
grind." And, if she pressed him in a jealous fashion, his justi-
fications might resemble those of a young artist explaining
his necessity to sketch nude models. Of course, there would be
strict rules forbidding dalliance between scientist and volunteer after hours. But, should they happen to run into one another in the cafeteria, each would keep his conversation casual,

6 5

trying not to allude to those more cataclysmic events of a few hours before. Mindful of his professional integrity, the scientist would have to guard against prideful thoughts that he knew her, if not better, at least more microscopically than those nearest her. Most troublesome of his self-appointed tasks, it seems to me, would be his effort to prevent his research from invading his own ordinary erotic life, particularly if it were worried by the usual frustrations. In this regard, he would be indeed heroic to withstand the temptation of comparing his mate's response to those unspecific, yet perfectly formed, consummations of the laboratory.

Again, if these imaginings have any truth, how may we characterize the ideal scientist in research of this immediate order? First of all, he would have to believe, far more than the volunteers, in a "basic science" approach to sex. This is not to say that he would consider the practice of sex a possible science, even though his practice might eventually be informed by his scientific theories. But it would have to be an article of faith for him that the visible, palpable reactions of the organs themselves, regardless of whatever human or inhuman context they might occur in, would speak a clear, unambiguous truth to all who cared to heed. In his hierarchy of beliefs, these reactions would take precedence in every sense. The questions we are apt to ask about human affairs, not excluding lust, ordinarily have to do with appropriateness, affection, and the like—in other words, right or wrong, good or bad, judged in human terms. On the other hand, the Ideal Sexologist, as he presses his eye to his research, finds another variety of drama—inordinately complicated in its comings and goings, crises and resolutions—with its own requirements of right and wrong, good and bad, all writ very small in terms of "droplets" and "engorgements" and "contractions." The will of the Ideal Sexologist seems different from the will of the Lady of the Laboratory, but it may be that the opposition is more illusory than actual. The latter wills orgasm through physical manipulation. Certainly the sexologist supports and approves her willing, such sexual promptness being ideal for laboratory study. However, while his approval may be invented by his will, it is by no means the most important expression of his will. As a scientist, his will must be given to the systematic inspection of the sexual response of the "human female," literally portrayed. To this end he persists in his gadgetry, always at the expense of any imaginative grasp of the occasion. His will to be a scientist requires his further commitment to any number of willful enterprises; in the present circumstance he finds it necessary to will his own body to be unresponsive—not merely to the events on the laboratory table, but to any fictional construction of these events his imagination might contrive, because imagination, at least in this arena, is his opponent in his pursuit of science. On the surface his dilemma may seem a familiar one, being comparable to older ascetic ventures, particularly of the Eastern yoga variety. But the sexologist's task is actually more difficult: asceticism is not his goal—the very nature of his enterprise points in an opposite direction. He wishes indifference, which he can invoke at will: it may be the project that demands his not responding, but—as we shall see later—it may be other moments, unofficial and unscientific, which seem to call forth his willed lack of response. The will not to respond and the will to respond are related possibilities of the will. In this sense, the Lady of the Laboratory and the Ideal Sexologist are collaborators rather than opponents. Of course, I speak in ideal terms—whether these ideals can be achieved is another matter. But, if the Lady of the Laboratory is a latter day Queen of Courtly Love, then our Ideal Sexologist is the modern Sir Galahad, and together—separately or commingled—they rule our dreams of what should be.

Let us remind ourselves that most of us could not hope to qualify for this research—either as volunteers or as scientists.

But this does not mean the differences are great between us and them. True, compared to ours, their lives have an over-sized quality, and true, they are in the vanguard. But, in a real sense our fleshly home is that laboratory. Whatever room we choose for our lovemaking we shall make into our own poor laboratory, and nothing that is observed or undergone in the real laboratory of science is likely to escape us. At this stage, is there any bit of sexology that is not in the public domain, or at least potentially so for those who can read? Whatever detail the scientific will appropriates about sex rapidly becomes an injunction to be imposed on our bodies. But, it is not long before these impositions lose their arbitrary and alien character and begin to change our actual experience of our bodies. Unfortunately, our vision of the ideal experience tends to be crudely derived from the failure of our bodies to meet these imperatives.

Our residence in the laboratory is recent: really only since the turn of the century has the act of sex been interviewed, witnessed, probed, measured, timed, taped, photographed, and judged. Before the age of sexology, objectifications of the sexual act were to be found in pornography and the brothel, both illicit, both pleasurable in purpose, both suggesting the relatively limited manner in which will—given absolute dominion —could be joined to sexual pleasure. However else the Marquis de Sade may be read, he at least offered the most exhaustive inventory yet seen of techniques for exploiting the pleasure of the body's several parts, if one wholeheartedly put one's will to it. As a moralist, he seemed to say, Why our particular rules? What if there were no limits? More recently, yet still before sexology, it was possible for shy erotomaniacs, disguised as greengrocers, to visit brothels, there to peek at the antics of the inmates. The bolder ones could join the sport. When the performance reached its final gasp our tradesmen, now satiated, would slink back to the propriety and privacy of their own quarters, convinced their ordinary domestic world was discreetly separate from the world of the peephole which they paid to enter. In fact, or so it seemed, the separateness of these two worlds heightened the erotic possibilities of each. The emancipation which sexology enforced gradually blurred this distinction, making it unclear whether each home had become its own brothel, or whether every brothel had become more like home. The truth is that sexology eventually not only blurred the distinction, but by housing us all in laboratories, made both the brothel and pornography less exciting dwellings for our erotic investigations.

When last we left our pathetic lovers, I suggested that as their self-pity and bitterness mounted, they might—in desperation—turn to adultery. Yet even for the person who believes himself to be without scruples, adultery—in fact or fantasy—is difficult to arrange, exhausting to maintain. Requiring, as it does, at least two persons and two wills, this illicit encounter risks the danger of further pathos. But, if we heed our laboratory drama carefully, we can see that there is another possibility preferable to adultery. According to the lesson of the laboratory, there is only one perfect orgasm, if by "perfect" we mean one wholly subject to its owner's will, wholly indifferent to human contingency or context. Clearly, the perfect orgasm is the orgasm achieved on one's own. No other consummation offers such certainty and, moreover, avoids the messiness that attends most human affairs. The onanist may choose the partner of his dreams who very probably will be the Lady of the Laboratory, or he may have his orgasm without any imagined partner. In either case, he is both scientist and experimental subject, science and sex now being nicely joined. In his laboratory room, he may now abstract his sexual parts from his whole person, inspect their anatomic particularities, and observe and enjoy the small physiologic events he knows best how to control. True, this solitary experience may leave him empty and ashamed. But, as a citizen of his times, he will try to counter this discomfort by reminding himself that sexology and psychoanalysis have assured him that masturbation is a morally indifferent matter. As a true modern, he tells himself that it is not as good as what two people have, but that does not make it bad. Superstitious people of other ages thought it drove one crazy, but he knows better; he knows that the real threat to *his* sanity is unrelieved sexual tension. In fact—he may decide—were it not for certain neurotic Victorian traces he has not managed to expunge from his psyche, he could treat the matter as any other bodily event and get on with his business. So we must not be too harsh with our pathetic lovers, if they take refuge in solitary pleasures— even if they come to prefer them to the frustrations of sexual life together. Nor should we be too surprised if such solitary pleasure becomes the ideal by which all mutual sex is measured—and found wanting.

Let us now turn to the phenomenon being inspected and celebrated in our laboratory—the phenomenon which contributes most of all to our lovers' impasse. Of all the discoveries sexology has made, the female orgasm remains the most imposing in its consequences. De Tocqueville's prediction of life between the sexes in America[10] might not have been so sanguine, could he have anticipated first, the discovery of sexology and psychoanalysis, and second, their discovery of the female orgasm.

In the second half of the nineteenth century, Western man

[10] ". . . I never observed that the women of America consider conjugal authority as an unfortunate usurpation of their rights, or that they thought themselves degraded by submitting to it. It appeared to me, on the contrary, that they attach a sort of pride to the voluntary surrender of their will. . . . Though their lot is different, they consider both of them as beings of equal value. . . . If I were asked . . . to what the singular prosperity and growing strength of that people ought mainly to be attributed, I should reply: To the superiority of their women." Alexis de Tocqueville, *Democracy in America* (New York: Alfred A. Knopf, 1945), Vol. II, pp. 212–214.

began to see nature in a new and utilitarian way as a variety of energies, hitherto unharnessed, which could now be tamed and transformed into industrial servants and which, in turn, would fashion never-ending progress and prosperity. The health of the machine, powered by steam and electricity, and the sickness of the machine, if those energies were misdirected or obstructed, were obsessive considerations of the period. It was entirely appropriate to regard the human body as still another natural object with many of the vicissitudes of the machine: this had always been medicine's privilege. But, for the first time, the scientists, in their intoxication, could forget the duality previous centuries knew: namely, that the body is both a natural object and not a natural object. Once it was decided that the dominant energy of the human machine was sex, the new science of sexology was born. With the suppression of the second half of the dialectic, sexology and psychoanalysis could—with the assistance of the Romantics—claim the erotic life as their exclusive province, removing it from all the traditional disciplines, such as religion, philosophy, and literature, which had always concerned themselves with sex as human experience. Such qualities as modesty, privacy, reticence, abstinence, chastity, fidelity, and shame could now be questioned as rather arbitrary matters that interfered with the health of the sexual parts. In their place came an increasing assortment of objective terms like *ejaculatio praecox*, foreplay, forepleasure, and frigidity—all intended to describe, not human experience, but the behavior of the sexual parts. The quite preposterous situation arose in which the patient sought treatment for *ejaculatio praecox* or impotence, and the healer sought to find out whether he liked his partner.

If the Victorians found sex unspeakable for the wrong reasons, the Victorian sexologists found it wrongly speakable. (To what extent Victorian prudery was actually modesty or reticence, I cannot say. It has become habitual for us to regard Victorian lovemaking as an obscenity.) Science is usually democratic, and since sex now belonged to science, whatever facts or assumptions were assembled had immediately to be transmitted to the people, there to invade their daily life. Writing of the Kinsey Report, Lionel Trilling finds—correctly, I believe—a democratic motive for the study:

> In speaking of its motives, I have in mind chiefly its impulse toward acceptance and liberation, its broad and generous desire for others that they be not harshly judged. . . . The Report has the intention of habituating its readers to sexuality in all its manifestations; it wants to establish, as it were, a democratic pluralism of sexuality. . . . This generosity of mind . . . goes with a nearly conscious aversion from making intellectual distinctions, almost as if out of the belief that an intellectual distinction must inevitably lead to a social discrimination or exclusion.[11]

If we disregard Kinsey's scientific pretensions, we still must recognize his eminence as an arbiter of sexual etiquette. Like the lexicographer who finds his sanction in usage, Kinsey discovers his authority in practice: his democratic message is that we all do—or should do—more or less the same things in bed. And, any notion lovers retain from an older tradition that what they have together is private and unique is effectively disproved by his cataloguing of sexual matters, providing they join him in equating behavior with experience. As a fitting disciple of Kinsey, Masters actualizes the "pluralism of sexuality" within the democratic unit of the laboratory and enlarges behavior to include the more minute physiological developments which, too, should belong to every citizen.

The political clamor for equal rights for the woman at the turn of the century could not fail to join with sexology to endow her with an orgasm, equal in every sense to the male

---

[11] Lionel Trilling, "The Kinsey Report," in *The Liberal Imagination* (New York: Doubleday Anchor Books, 1954), pp. 232–233.

orgasm. In fact, Freud went so far as to stipulate two female orgasms, clitoral and vaginal, the latter clearly superior. (It was not many years ago that an anatomist demonstrated that there were as many nerve endings in the clitoris as in the penis.) It was agreed that, just as she was entitled to the vote, she was entitled to her orgasm. Moreover, if she were deprived of such release, her perturbation would be as unsettling to her nervous system as the frustration of orgasm was thought to be for the man. Equal rights were to be erotically consummated in simultaneous orgasm. On the one hand, it was unhealthful for her to be deprived of orgasm, and, on the other hand, psychoanalysis decreed that an important sign of her maturity as a woman was her ability to achieve orgasm. In other words, without orgasm she was neurotic to begin with, or neurotic to end with.

Though simultaneous orgasm seemed to be a necessary consequence of equal rights, the problem remained that, in matters of lust, more than a decree or amendment was required for such an achievement. True, the sexologists were most generous with instruction, but each citizen has had to discover over and over again the degree to which he is caught in the futile struggle to will what cannot be willed—at the same time that he senses the real absurdity of the whole willful enterprise. The lover learns, as his indoctrination progresses, to observe uneasily and even to resist his rush of pleasure, if it seems he is to be premature. When no amount of resolution can force his pleasure to recede, he learns to suffer his release and then quickly prod himself to an activity his body's exhaustion opposes. In other words, he learns to take his moment in stride, so to speak, omitting the deference these moments usually call forth, and without breaking stride get to his self-appointed, and often fatiguing, task of tinkering with his mate—always hopeful that his ministrations will have the appearance of affection. While she is not likely to be deceived by such dutiful manipulation, she nevertheless wishes for both their sakes that her body, at least, will be deluded into fulfilling its franchise. Still, it cannot be easy for her to ignore the irony that her right to orgasm may perhaps depend for realization upon her willingness to be diddled like a perverse underwater edible whose shell refuses to be pried open.

As far as I know, little attention was paid to the female orgasm before the era of sexology. Where did the sexologists find it? Did they discover it or invent it? Or both? I realize it may seem absurd to raise such questions about events as unmistakable as those witnessed in our laboratory. But I cannot believe that previous centuries were not up to our modern delights; nor can I believe it was the censorship imposed by religion which suppressed the supreme importance of the female orgasm. My guess, which is not subject to laboratory proof, is that the female orgasm was always an occasional, though not essential, part of woman's whole sexual experience. I also suspect that it appeared with regularity or predictability only during masturbation, when the more human qualities of her life with her mate were absent. Further, her perturbation was unremarkable and certainly bearable when orgasm did not arrive, for our lovers had not yet been enlightened as to the disturbances resulting from the obstruction or distortion of sexual energies. At this stage, her orgasm had not yet been abstracted and isolated from the totality of her pleasures, and enshrined as the meaning and measure of her erotic life. She was content with the mystery and variety of her difference from man and, in fact, would not have had it otherwise. Much that I have said, if we leave aside the erotomanias that have always been with us, applies to the male of previous centuries. For him, too, the moment of orgasm was not abstracted in its objective form from the whole of his erotic life and then idealized. He, too, preferred the mystery of difference, the impact of human contingency, becoming obsessed with the sheer anatomy and mechanics of orgasm only when all else was missing, as in masturbation.

Theological parallelism is a treacherous hobby, especially when we deal with flagrantly secular movements. Nevertheless, the manner in which lovers now pursue their careers as copulating mammals, adopting whatever new refinements sexology devises, covering their faces yet exposing their genitals, may remind us of older heresies which, through chastity or libertinism, have pressed toward similar goals; one heretical cult went so far as to worship the serpent in the Garden of Eden. But the difference between these older heresies and modern science—and there is a large one—must be attributed to the nature of science itself, which, by means of its claims to objectivity—if we accept such evidence as the Lambeth Conference, can invade religion and ultimately all of life to a degree denied the older heresies. So, with the abstraction, objectification, and idealization of the female orgasm, we have come to the last and perhaps most important clause to the contract which binds our lovers to their laboratory home, there to will the perfection on earth that cannot be willed, there to suffer the pathos that follows all such strivings toward heaven on earth.

4

DESPAIR AND
THE LIFE OF
SUICIDE

Gabriel Marcel has written: ". . . the fact that suicide is always possible is the essential starting point of any genuine metaphysical thought."[1] It might equally be said that the possibility of suicide will always oppose psychiatry's efforts to rid itself of metaphysical concern. For once that possibility disrupts the civilized and ordinary boundaries of psychotherapy, every technical category loses its ordered place in our thinking and must be questioned with a new urgency or exploited in a manner that robs it of whatever truthful meaning it may have earned. What I have chosen to discuss here is—if I may be permitted this irony—the life of suicide, as distinguished from the act itself.

Martin Buber once remarked: "The act of suicide—it is a trapdoor which suddenly springs open. What else can one say?" Well, one can say a great deal, to judge from psychiatric

[1] Gabriel Marcel, *The Philosophy of Existentialism* (New York: The Citadel Press, 1961), p. 26.

literature. But, it is my impression that while to the man who kills himself the act of suicide may be a trapdoor suddenly sprung, to the analyst it seems rather to resemble a psychological staircase, leading step by logical step to an inescapable culmination. Although I don't wish to force the image, I must remark that whether this staircase goes down or up, it must always be traveled backwards. Confronted with the fact of suicide, the analyst must construct his explanation in reverse, laying motive upon motive (hostility is favored here), and strategy upon strategy, until he reaches some final necessity. Having arrived at the end of his staircase, he may then retrace his steps forward, issuing those kitchen prescriptions for the heading-off of the act with which we are all familiar.

I would suggest that this staircase, though a far more reassuring and manageable structure than the suicide's own trapdoor, exists principally in the analyst's head, not in the real world. On the other hand, the world is full of trapdoors, even though the only ones we can be sure of are those which have already sprung open. The invention of the staircase is hardly surprising; a trapdoor offers very little to an investigator bent on explanation, and, by extension, recipes for prevention. But it is my suspicion that the staircase leads us, not to greater understanding, but merely away from the issue. It prevents us, after all, right at the outset, from even considering the possibility that the act of suicide is not the final move in a chain of causation—that perhaps it is not *caused* at all, in a psychological sense. Naturally, this is not an agreeable proposition to the psychologist, who tends, understandably, to feel somewhat panicked if suddenly robbed of his basic tenet and tool, causation. Be that as it may, I feel that there is a more fruitful approach, even for psychiatrists, to the issue of suicide than the construction of causes out of motives. And that is: to leave aside, for the moment, the act itself, and to contemplate what I have called "the life of suicide"—which must be seen, not as the situation or state of mind which *leads to* the act, but that situation in which the act-as-possibility, quite apart from whether it eventually occurs or not, has a life of its own.

It is part of our most profound—or metaphysical—awareness of ourselves, as Marcel has pointed out, to acknowledge that the possibility of suicide belongs to the human condition. We know this and must live with it, in much the same way as we know and must live with the fact that sin and evil are no strangers to our nature. But the awareness that it is possible for us to kill ourselves does not lead us to embrace suicide, any more than does the awareness that we are sinners prompt us to go forth and sin. For the man who is caught up in what I have called "the life of suicide," however, the possibility of being the author of his own death exercises a demonic and seductive fascination over him. This fascination takes different forms. There is a certain kind of person for whom the idea of suicide is a secret and cherished solution to any difficulty life may throw across his path. Suicide is the ace up his sleeve (revealed to no one), the secret possession of which shapes his response to any and every problem. Such a man confronts his life whispering to himself, "If I can't find a better job, I'll kill myself. If my son won't confide in me, if my daughter flunks her final exams, if my wife forgets my birthday just one more time—I'll kill myself." This man, although caught up in one form of the life of suicide, is not, I think, in despair. Despair, which arises only in someone capable of some seriousness toward his life and himself, is literally beyond such a person. His secret scheming with the concealed trump of suicide altogether robs any event in his life—and quickly enough his entire life—of meaning, but without imposing upon him the necessity of acknowledging or dealing with meaninglessness. And, because concealment is so vital to his "advantage," as he conceives it, and therefore his deviousness and dishonesty so virtually impossible to penetrate, he is, I believe, the most difficult of all potential suicides to treat—or help in any way. Though not suffering the estrangement of true despair, this man is actually more separated from the world and his fellows than the despairer in his worst agonies of despairing isolation. I will return to this question of estrangement, but at this point I would like to contrast this form of the life of suicide that I have described with a form that we more commonly encounter: the suicidal preoccupation of the man who *is* in despair.

Suicide finds no more fertile soil for its intrigues than despair—that "sickness unto death" in which, as Kierkegaard observed, we long to die and cannot. It is the middle years that are most vulnerable to the claims of this sickness of spirit, which now radically questions all we have been, at the same time scorning the solace formerly sought in the future, making who we are to become the most oppressive of questions. As both the workings and visages of the flesh falter and wither, all crude preconceptions of immortality are shattered, giving way to a brooding—and equally crude—apprehension of the finitude of our earthly stay. Gradually—or even suddenly —there emerges the realization, "For better or worse, that was it. There never was a second chance." Time past now isolates itself as an alien, often perverse accomplice, sometimes accepting, but more often refusing, memory's overtures. What cannot be remembered robs us of goods that seem rightfully ours, so that memory turns feverish and willful in its pursuit of the past—the past we thought we owned when it was the present, and assumed we would continue to own in the future. What we would remember eludes us; what we would forget we now remember with a fresh and painful clarity we never before knew. All those cruelties, deceits, and betrayals which we inflicted on the human order disclose themselves as wounds that would not and cannot heal. Of such real guilt Martin Buber wrote:

A man stands before us who, through acting or failing to act, has burdened himself with a guilt or has taken part in a community guilt, and now, after years or decades, is again and again visited by the memory of his guilt. Nothing of the genesis of his illness is concealed from him if he is only willing no longer to conceal from himself the guilt character of that active or passive occurrence. What takes possession of him ever again has nothing to do with any parental or social reprimand, and if he does not have to fear an earthly retribution and does not believe in a heavenly one, no court, no punishing power exists that can make him anxious. Here there rules the one penetrating insight—the one insight capable of penetrating into the impossibility of recovering the original point of departure and the irreparability of what has been done, and that means the real insight into the irreversibility of lived time, a fact that shows itself unmistakably in the starkest of all human perspectives, that concerning one's own death. From no standpoint is time so perceived as a torrent as from the vision of the self in guilt. Swept along in this torrent, the bearer of guilt is visited by the shudder of identity with himself. I, he comes to know, I, who have become another, am the same.[2]

As despair deepens, what had meaning now seems meaningless; what seemed meaningless is fraught with meaning. There develops an ever-widening rift between the despairer and the person he was, between him and the world in which he lived. Though estranged from the world and the self who formerly dwelt in that world, he is at the same time—out of his craving for reconciliation—now wholly absorbed with that world and that self. Envy and pride conspire to increase the rift. Strangers passing him on the street appear to him transfigured by their thoughtless possession of just what he has lost: the sheer, taken-for-granted ordinariness of life. In the misery of the envy they incite in him, he isolates and exalts that quality of life that can flourish only in disregard: a sense of belong-

[2] Martin Buber, "Guilt and Guilt Feelings," *Psychiatry*, 20 (1957), 116.

ing to whatever worlds one lives in that is both concrete and casual. Finding himself outside his own world, he discovers that he is unequal to it, and he yearns to sever whatever ties still bind him to this world to which he no longer belongs. Fitfully he contemplates other worlds—the simple job, the monastery, the tropical island, the sick room. But, he flinches as he imagines addressing himself to the machinery of preparation, explanation, and farewell that such a flight requires, and he realizes further that no haven offers a promise of honoring his passport on arrival. Though he may believe himself the most miserably humbled of men, it is not humility but pride that rules his imagination in this enterprise. His visions of escape from his tormenting world are apt to be rather grand in scope, and turn about such possibilities as remote lands and the monastic life. Taking a job as a shoe clerk does not occur to him—though it might be more in keeping with the humility he ascribes to himself. Within him, pride and despair, which since the earliest stages of his affliction have found themselves natural and powerful partners, each encouraging and supporting the claims and strategies of the other, now discover in the despairer's yearning for escape merely one more invitation to exercise their formidable collaborative gifts and assume command. Inspired by his despair, his pride now invents in its own image the possible alternatives to the world that surrounds him, excluding him. It may happen that he perseveres, and reaches his island, or the disturbed ward of some closer-by institution, thus shutting out the world that had shut the door on him. Yet what he cannot shut out, what accompanies him on any journey he makes, is his own despair. And, with his despair, his overweening pride. His despair is not in the possession of the world, nor can he abandon it as he can abandon a city, a job, or a marriage, and flee to some uncontaminated place. His despair is his alone; it travels with him and lives where he lives; and, whether he stays or flees, he must eventually discover that it responds—in any significant sense—as little to geographical as to stylistic change. Its indifference to maneuvers is absolute.

Because intercourse with his fellows only reminds him of what he no longer has, he slowly loses the power to be with other human beings—even as their physical presence grows ever more essential. To some degree he is conscious that his mounting self-absorption is accompanied by a dwindling perception of others. What concern he manages he must will: thus does he leap from his reveries to arrange his features in some imitation of interest and animation, to open doors, light others' cigarettes, to "participate"—usually in some stilted, feverish way that constitutes the best performance to which his will alone can move him—in "the scene," in "a social situation," where his presence in a group of people seems to require certain ordinary capacities he finds he now suddenly and totally lacks. Dreading that others will recognize what he already knows and abandon him, he feels compelled to declare some disability that will legitimize his distracted self-absorption in the eyes of those about him, in the hope that they will extend the same tolerance toward him that any invalid may rightfully expect. Like the sinner in *The Fall*, by Camus, the despairer knows that "the essential is being able to permit oneself everything, even if, from time to time, one has to profess vociferously one's own infamy."[3] In this state, he experiences an overwhelming longing to confess—but what he confesses is not his wickedness, which would be a proper subject for confession and which might involve him in some redeeming attitude toward both his confession and his life. Instead, what he wishes to confess is his worthlessness—his infirmity. Such a confession is spurious, of course; it does not touch on issues of forgiveness or repentance that are relevant to his condition. In "confessing" infirmity, what the despairer

[3] Albert Camus, *The Fall* (New York: Alfred A. Knopf, 1957), p. 141.

would coerce—and here his willfulness is quite brutal—is an acknowledgment of his disease in terms that are almost physical. I find no mystery in the eagerness of those in despair to secure a physical diagnosis—say depression—and then offer themselves to pills or electric shock or lobotomy—anything that will spare them real contrition. But, more mysterious to me is the willingness of those of our calling to accept the more demonic terms of despair, to conspire to relieve the despairer of his humanity through chemical, electrical, or surgical means.

Even in such a brief account of the landscape of despair, it must be clear that despair—potentially at least—is both destroying and renewing. With this double potentiality in mind, T. S. Eliot has addressed himself to the despairer in this manner:

I said to my soul, be still, and wait without hope
For hope would be hope for the wrong thing; wait without love
For love would be love of the wrong thing; there is yet faith
But the faith and the love and the hope are all in the waiting.
Wait without thought, for you are not ready for thought:
So the darkness shall be light, and the stillness the dancing.[4]

While we may not share the author's rather Eastern reliance on the waiting itself as the way out of despair, still we must acknowledge how difficult it is for the despairer to still his soul—or his mind. While despair means literally the loss of hope, the movements of despair are frantically directed toward hope; but the hope born of despair may turn to the prescriptions of the isolated will. Spurning the self-illumination arising from true humility, despairing hope concerns itself pridefully with certainties. Even the certainty of hopelessness may paradoxically appear as a form of hope, promising to make reason-

[4] T. S. Eliot, "East Coker," *Four Quartets* (New York: Harcourt, Brace, 1943), p. 15.

able what is unreasonable, namely hopelessness itself. The despairer may, at this opaque moment, be utterly convinced of the clarity of his vision, condemning the world that preceded his despair as no more than a sentimental insanity, a silly fabrication created by his own unwillingness to discern the harsh truth about this existence. It is as if his imagination, in its fullest sense, had abdicated, and now his will could apply itself to the task of reducing what is most human, to pursuing ever further the inevitability—and therefore the essential absurdity—of all that has been and all that will be. He now seems to himself, despite his melancholy, the most reasonable and forthright of men. Like Kirillov in Dostoyevsky's *The Possessed*, he proclaims, "I am just such a scoundrel as you, as all, not a decent man. There's never been a decent man anywhere . . . all the planet is a lie and rests on a lie and on mockery. So then, the very laws of the planet are a lie and the vaudeville of devils."[5] This is the realism of a truly macabre predictability. And a "vaudeville of devils" accurately describes the stale, repetitious, lifeless routines from which the despairer yearns to escape. Surprise and mystery have vanished from his view, if not from his experience. If he contemplates a visit with friends, he can no longer imagine the casual, the unexpected moment that might offer even momentary relief. No, instead he writes both scripts and concludes from his authorship that, since he knows what would happen, there is no reason for making such a visit. But, if life itself should provide a casual moment, even with a stranger, which quite cuts through his self-absorption, wholly transforming his mood, he has no capacity to celebrate this moment. In fact, he will disown or conceal the moment, rather than allow it to question his dismal certainty, and he thus learns cagily to protect his state from life's interventions. Even

[5] Fyodor Dostoyevsky, *The Possessed* (New York: The Modern Library, 1936), pp. 625–629.

the rational or logical steps to his conclusions, which strike him as utterly convincing, may turn shabby if exposed to the light of discourse. So, pride urges him to keep his own counsel, even though it mean his death. Thus does the despairer appear before us to ask that most extraordinary and truly diabolical question—especially when addressed to a psychotherapist—"Is there any good in talking?" After this, we may recover our composure and succeed in engaging him imaginatively, so that real talk, does, after all, begin to come about. Despite his absolute certainty of a few moments before that even momentary relief from the torment of despair was no longer possible, his despairing self-absorption may yield to forthright interest in the subject at hand, a yielding which goes beyond mere distraction. Relief has, in spite of everything, actually been granted him; his despairing certainty has been exposed to the real world of discourse and proved false. We might even say that a minor miracle has occurred. What are we to answer then, when, as the hour nears its end, our patient or friend, preparing to take his leave, turns to us and asks, "But haven't you something *useful* to say to me—something I can use after I leave here?" If there is an answer to this question, it has not occurred to me. I wish to comment only on one of its most curious aspects: the man who spoke these words was one who had recently been in despair and would, very likely, soon be in despair again. Yet, by this question, which could occur only to a despairing mind, despair reasserted its claim on him, still without forcing upon him the anguish that is its customary companion. Contained within his question is the reminder that such fleeting moments of relief are all very well, but after all truth is truth and logic is logic, and by truth of course he means despairing truth, and by logic he means despairing logic. This is to say that what he wishes to take with him to counter his despairing certainties are other certainties, maxim-like morsels, prescriptive in nature, which, like pills, will offer him some comfort when the pain returns. Almost while still celebrating the wonder of his renewal, he has with his question submitted himself again to despair.

The fascination of suicide to a despairing mind lies in the fact that it offers a demonic solution for every anguished, humbling, and potentially renewing claim which despair may make. As Marcel has written, the possibility of suicide may provide the beginnings of metaphysical thought. However, when an absorption with suicide possesses the despairer, it becomes—as Marcel has said—"the expression of another much more profound and more hidden possibility, the possibility of a spiritual denial of self, or, what comes to the same thing, of an impious and demonic affirmation of self which amounts to a radical rejection of being."[6] We have, I think, no more desperate illustration of the manner in which suicide violates every human claim which may exist in despair than Kirillov's explanation of his suicide:

Man has done nothing but invent God so as to go on living, and not kill himself . . . I can't understand how an atheist could know there is no God and not kill himself on the spot. To recognize that there is no God and not to recognize at the same instant that one is God oneself is an absurdity, else one would certainly kill oneself. If you recognize it you are sovereign, and then you won't kill yourself but will live in the greatest glory. But one, the first, must kill himself, for else who will begin and prove it? So I must certainly kill myself, to begin and prove it. Now I am only a god against my will and I am unhappy, because I am *bound* to assert my will. All are unhappy because all are afraid to express their will. Man has hitherto been so unhappy and so poor because he has been afraid to assert his will in the highest point and has shown his self-will only in little things, like a schoolboy. I am awfully unhappy, for I'm awfully afraid. Terror is the curse of man . . . But I will assert my will, I am bound to believe that I don't believe. I will begin and will make an end of it and open the door,

[6] Gabriel Marcel, *The Mystery of Being: 2. Faith & Reality* (Chicago: Henry Regnery, 1960), p. 194.

and will save. That's the only thing that will save mankind and will recreate the next generation physically; for with his present physical nature man can't get on without his former God, I believe. For three years I've been seeking for the attribute of my godhead and I've found it; the attribute of my godhead is self-will! That's all I can do to prove in the highest point my independence and my new terrible freedom. For it is very terrible. I am killing myself to prove my independence and my new terrible freedom.[7]

This quotation is a combination of two speeches of Kirillov's that occur close together in the course of a dialogue several pages long, a series of assertions that seem to me to constitute an excellent example of certain aspects of the suicidal despair I have been discussing. As I examine Kirillov's declarations, I will try to make clear my own understanding of what is happening in this passage, and what significance it may have for our consideration of despair and the life of suicide.

As Kirillov expounds on the purpose and necessity of his suicide, the voice we hear seems hardly to belong to a person. Or, if we can imagine a person to be present, it must strike us that this person's singular life as human being is almost wholly submerged in a sea of generalizations about the human condition and the existence of God. Both the tone and the substance of these generalizations exhibit the certainty of a creature with godlike pretensions, while at the same time testifying, by the forced nature of the logic, that this certainty is constantly assailed by fear and doubt. And, further, that uncertainty is unnaturally frightening to such a mind; in its fear of any sort of question, it leaps to answer the wrong questions. Again, Eliot's lines come to mind: Kirillov is precisely a man unable to still his soul—or his mind, which, indeed, has become merely the reasoning function (however impaired its power to reason) of his sovereign will. The very thing he

---

[7] Dostoyevsky, *op. cit.*, pp. 629–630.

cannot do is wait. Willfully he hopes, and, inevitably, his hope is hope for the wrong thing. Bereft of faith, yet lusting for faith, willfully he invents his own creed and embraces it with willful belief. He is indeed "not ready for thought," yet thought seems to be the only response his mind can imagine making to the despair which overwhelms it.

We should note that at no point—in this passage or in the course of the entire scene—does Kirillov admit, or indeed even begin to recognize, his own despair. This is the worst of all despairs in which, as Kierkegaard has written, the despairer does not know he is in despair. With that variety of logic that is born only in despair, he reasons that even though he might live on and on in "greatest glory" as God, he must be the first to kill himself in order to "prove" his divinity—or, more accurately, his immortality. Usually the despairer, as I mentioned earlier, learns to mask such demonic logic as this out of his prideful apprehension that any explicit exposure might reveal it as foolish, even absurd. But Kirillov, ignorant of his despair, fails to experience such apprehension; although not altogether confident of the truth of his assertions, neither his doubts nor his pain suggests to him the nature of his condition. What intervenes between the plentiful evidence of despair and his notice of such evidence is, of course, his will, which cunningly blocks his vision at every turn.

And, in this willed blindness toward his state of mind, he is incapable both of imagining, and certainly of contending, with such a real issue as guilt. There is little suggestion in his discourse of a human soul suspended in anguish and guilt over its own particular injuries to the human order. Being beyond remorse, all Kirillov can do is to call himself and all other men scoundrels, at the same time declaring the entire planet to be a mockery. That there might potentially be guilt, were he able to pursue real self-illumination, is suggested by his wish to save—not himself, but "mankind," even though all men be scoundrels. Out of his loss of faith, he perpetrates a familiar psychologism, strangely similar to Freud's view of religion: namely, that men have invented God in order to stay alive. Untroubled by any memory of other times when he must have deceived himself with other certainties, he now decrees without hesitation that if there is no God, then he must be God.

Not only is there no suggestion of guilt in Kirillov's proclamations, neither is there any intimation that he may have wrestled with—or even acknowledged—the terror roused in him by the idea of his own death. What we hear instead is the rather plaintive statement that he is unhappy and afraid. And, even the possibilities for self-illumination that might lie in this limited admission—were he able to hold himself still in the presence of such unhappiness and fear long enough to perceive some hint of their nature and meaning—are quickly dissipated in the generalization that "terror is the curse of man."

At only one point in this passage does Kirillov seem perilously close to an encounter with the real nature of his condition—an encounter which might force him to abandon his despairing logic. His abrupt assertion that his suicide is "the only thing that will save mankind and will recreate the next generation physically; for with his present physical nature man can't get on without his former God, I believe," contradicts the primary assumption on which his entire argument has rested up to this point: namely, that man could get on without God perfectly well, if it were only proved to him once and for all that God didn't exist. He seems suddenly to have stumbled upon an alarming and utterly unmanageable truth: man's need for God is contained in his very physical nature— his mortality, his helplessness to alter the absolute necessity of death. The fact that such a truth could have penetrated the fortifications that will has erected on every side of his awareness must mean that Kirillov, despite his claims to omniscience, has failed to convince himself with his own despairing reasoning. In the moment of his realization of this failure, and faced with the truth he has just perceived, his despair would seem to be on the brink of a crisis of exposure and self-illumination. But his will, rather than accept such a defeat, commands avoidance of this crisis, and presses him instead to outwit the moment with the most extreme and bizarre assertion he has yet made: since man's "physical recreation" is necessary to liberate him from his need for God, such "physical recreation" is precisely what Kirillov's suicide is designed to achieve.

The principal attribute of his godhead, he has discovered, is "self-will," by which he means the naked will directed toward the self—an unconditional Nietzschean will, which we might term willfulness, or perhaps pride, and which suggests the "demonic affirmation of self" of which Marcel has spoken. Kirillov will not entertain the possibility that such "self-will" might have landed him in his suicidal despair. Instead, he asserts the demonic principle that man has been unhappy because he has been afraid to be willful enough. Therefore, he will prove his independence and his "new terrible freedom" through the "supreme" act of "self-will," namely, suicide. This is to say that if, out of cowardice, he has failed himself and others, he will now prove his courage, not by contending in fear and trembling with the tumultuous questions of his existence and thus finding his life, but by ending his life. What never occurs to him is that by means of this very concept of "self-will" his whole argument has—perhaps not in terms of its own peculiar logic, but certainly in relation to truth—turned itself on its head. Instead of seeing "self-will" as his affliction, he conceives it as his godhead, and the instrument of his self-realization. Instead of seeing that his sovereign "self-will" enslaves every human aspect of his intelligence, he imagines it as the key to his "terrible freedom." Instead of recognizing "self-will" as the unmistakable clue to his demonic despair, he finds in it—by virtue of the extraordinary demands it imposes—the supreme heroism of his calling, justifying and explaining whatever fear, doubt, or pain may have threatened to shake his resolve. Instead of calling into question his manner —and, along with it, all his reasoning, the idea of "self-will" arrives in his mind as a sort of deus-ex-machina of logic, clarifying and confirming all that has gone before, setting upon the ordered whole its seal of authority and exaltation.

Having thus established the necessity of his suicide, Kirillov shoots himself. While perhaps a literary necessity, this is not really characteristic of the life of suicide, which may or may not terminate in the suicidal act itself.

Even before plots of suicide have begun to invade and absorb the despairer's subjectivity, his "self-will" may be exerted in destructive ways other than the "supreme" act of suicide. In an effort to breach his growing sense of estrangement, he may explode into a mania of self-assertive activity in which he would seem to be trying to overpower his anguish by exalting those more headstrong aspects of his nature which have brought him at last to despair. Alcohol or drugs may offer brutish assistance to this euphoric surge of personal motion, by means of which he tries to force his way back into the world. Of all the movements of despair, this clatter of the spirit is the most deafening and the most defeating, convincing no one, least of all himself. Deprived by this rush of will of the capacity for quieter moral discrimination, he now exposes himself to more and more opportunities for guilt which must also be overridden. Desperately hungry for reconciliation, he becomes increasingly estranged from those loved ones who might conceivably offer some relief, were it not being demanded of them. At this stage in his deprivation, he may turn unhappily to the task of documenting his estrangement by becoming a self-appointed, though miserable, expert on those deficiencies of his fellows that render them incapable of love—particularly the love toward him that would lighten his despair. While dimly conscious that his hectic state makes him unlovable, he maintains, in the midst of his fever, a wavering hope that the other will overwhelm his isolation with a burst of affection that will lighten his anguish and effectively dispute his despairing certainties. Naturally, he hesitates to reveal his perceptions of the manner in which the other has failed him, out of fear that he will make himself even more unlovable in the other's eyes. Nevertheless, his need may provoke him into an angry encounter in which, despite admissions of his own state, he still manages to list his charges. When love—or the inability to love—is examined in this objective manner as still another article of knowledge, every human being must acknowledge his failure. To defend one's capacity to love is a spiritual impossibility; it forces the loved one to objectify and therefore lose that which cannot be objectified, namely love itself. Often enough, the consequence of such an encounter is mutual despair. Even if the loved one manages not to fall into despair himself, he may still feel himself charged with the responsibility to love, so that in a self-conscious way he attempts to will what cannot be willed.

This phase of explosive activity will persist until the despairer's excesses become so outrageous to himself that a sudden—and shocking—perception of his own behavior plunges him into real self-loathing. In this state, he can no longer escape—or postpone—an acknowledgment of his despair, and, by virtue of this very acknowledgment, he may—still within despair—find his way toward the beginnings of self-illumination and renewal. But, should the possibility of such renewal elude him, he will now discover that this self-loathing has landed him in the bleakest, most naked realm of despair. The rush has subsided, leaving his despairing mind increasingly at the mercy of suicidal machinations. It is as though the will, which formerly asserted itself in activity, now turns to the invention of the details of one's self-destruction. At this stage, the body grows heavy and alien, so that the most ordinary physical tasks seem like monstrous obstacles, making the despairer wonder how he could ever have taken these matters for granted. He experiences his body as a ponderous affliction to which he longs to put an end. Yet, at the same time, his physical vanity is offended by this new imposition, so that often, in the midst of his suicidal ruminations, he will leave his chair to inspect his face in the mirror for any new wrinkles that may have appeared. At one moment, he may have decided on the exact date for his demise, while in the next he finds himself considering the purchase of a new and fashionable jacket. Such an outlandish mixture of the profound and the trivial—so characteristic of the life of suicide—does some disservice to his view of himself as a tragic figure. Increasingly, he comes to charge himself with duplicity, shallowness, even frivolity, and now it appears that the act of suicide is necessary to prove his seriousness. The absurdity and pathos of the life of suicide stem from the despairer's will to achieve—through suicide—his status as a moral human being. In a sense he asks, "How can I live decently in suicide?" Referring to the "radical rejection of being" that follows upon the "demonic affirmation of self" in the contemplation of suicide, Marcel adds, "that rejection is the final falsehood and absurdity; for it can exist only *through* someone who is; but, as it becomes embodied it develops into perverted being."[8] As a demonically constitutive symbol, suicide invokes every human concern. Inevitably the issue of courage is raised—not the courage to live in spite of despair, but the courage suicidally to put an end to all those cowardly hesitations that prevent the despairer from consummating his death. Brooding over the manner of his suicide, he searches again and again for the considerate way—the way that will

8 Marcel, *op. cit.*, p. 194.

make manifest his continuing solicitude for those who would be most damaged by his death. Timing becomes a weighty problem: it would be cruel to spoil the Christmas season for his family, selfish to disturb office business at this particular moment. (Let us note that this intricate solicitude toward others is, in truth, merely an absurd imitation of—or substitute for—his real guilt toward them and toward the whole human order, a guilt he is incapable of contending with directly.) The suicide note, since it must justify what cannot be justified, becomes a formidable and frustrating document as it is composed and recomposed in the despairer's mind, each new version suggesting the possibility that perhaps no note would be preferable to an unconvincing one: particularly since any note, depending on its imaginative adequacy, may expose to the despairer the essential absurdity of all he seeks to prove.

Even the extent of his suffering must be witnessed and authenticated by suicide. Repeatedly, he announces to himself that his state is unbearable. But, should he be challenged on this score—that is, how is he to know what is and what is not bearable for himself; in other words, what gives him this godlike certainty?—his answer, to himself at least, is that it must be unbearable, otherwise he would not be thinking of suicide. In solitude, this answer appears unassailable to the despairer. In fact, it may happen that the act of suicide seems to have become necessary to demonstrate how unendurable his pain is, in which case he commits suicide in order to prove it unendurable. Here, the despairer takes his own life to prove that he is not responsible for taking his own life. By definition, what is unendurable cannot be endured; therefore, his suicide is not a matter of choice but an externally determined response to a situation that has deprived him of choice. The flaw in this logical construct, of course, is that his definition of his condition as unendurable is very much a matter of choice, and thus, obviously, so is his suicide. What is interesting here is the

94

despairer's effort to deny the fact of choice and, by extension, to deny responsibility for his suicidal act. He does not say: "I am in great pain; I do not know how much longer I can contend with it; I do not know if I will be permitted some relief, or how much, or how soon, or if it will afford me any more than momentary comfort. But I choose to bear these uncertainties no further. I prefer to end my life of my own will and by my own hand. I choose this act and accept full responsibility for it." Though such a declaration contains a fairly accurate description of his situation, the despairer goes to some trouble to avoid such an acknowledgment of choice and responsibility. He must believe his suicide to be an inescapable fate imposed on him from without. Why? Is it perhaps possible that, even in the grip of his despair, he has not lost contact with his more human self, and the human truths his despair strives to deny—has not lost contact to such a degree that he no longer conceives suicide as a demonic act? Indeed, because he *does* recognize its nature, he shrinks from confronting the actual role of choice in his act. Even his despair will not allow him such an unholy embrace of moral grotesquerie as suicide. Were he capable of acknowledging the nature of this unholy embrace, and his responsibility in submitting to it, his despair—and his despairing estrangement from the world of the human—would be complete. The fact that his despair, instead of prompting this acknowledgment, labors to deny it altogether, to persuade him of his role as a helpless, and therefore blameless, victim; this fact suggests that in an important sense despair, by its very nature, is incapable of wholly fulfilling itself. As I remarked earlier, despair seems to afflict only those whose relation to life is a serious and potentially responsible one. It seems to me that those who are vulnerable to the worst torments of despair are also those who —because of what they were before falling into despair, and still, in the clutches of despair, potentially are—are seldom able quite to reach the demonic affirmation of self and the radical rejection of being toward which their despair strains. In some sense, the despairer moves hazardously, despite distractions and entrenchment, toward a tragic, often excessively tragic, position in regard to the inauthentic in his life and in his relations with others. In other words, through his objectifications he may arrive at an extreme and radical concern over the very center of his being, creating in this way an abyss too wide and too deep for easy bridging. The very strategies of despair, and especially the logical strategies involved in the contemplation of suicide, reveal that there is some connection still linking them to life-outside-despair—perhaps only imagined, but imagined still—that despair is unable to sever. Despair would not be so anguished a condition as it is were it as wholly and hopelessly estranged as it believes itself to be.

There is one last clause to the pact suicide makes with despair: suicide appears to offer a means of contending with the necessity and all the attending uncertainties of one's own death. What Buber has written of guilt applies equally to the person in despair: potentially he is permitted "the real insight into the irreversibility of lived time, a fact that shows itself unmistakably in the starkest of all human perspectives, that concerning one's own death." Opposing this insight, suicide promises, through an act of will, to resolve the terrors of mortality that in despair are so overwhelming. Death itself is certain; but how, when, where, in what manner, under what conditions, with what serenity or wild ravings, and *how soon* —this knowledge is not granted us. There is, however, one way in which a man may attain it, and by so doing "cheat" death, become its master by mastering its uncertainties—and this way is to stage and execute his own death, at the time, place, and in the manner of his own choosing. But, once embarked on this enterprise—or the contemplation of this enterprise—he becomes absorbed in the scene itself. As though carelessly overlooking the inevitable climax of the action: death, *his* death, he focuses his attention upon the staging of the act; he reviews and evaluates the methods available to him; in his imagination he lives and relives the discovery scene— at which in reality he can hardly expect to be present. And yet, in effect he must expect to be present, if through suicide he intends to master the terrors of death, because such terrors belong to life. Although the strategies involved in the attainment of this mastery can succeed only by luring his attention away from the real issue of his own death, their success is almost always incomplete and intermittent. Since his death is, after all, a detail of action inescapably necessary to his scenario —the single act about which his entire dramatic construction turns—its ultimate significance is not likely to remain safely hidden behind his busy concern with an endless variety of production problems; from time to time it rudely assaults his awareness, and in those moments he realizes all too clearly that the mastery suicide seemed to offer him was a cheat and a fake. But, each time this dreadful moment arrives, he wrenches away from it and fastens his imagination again on the fictional representation of his death, in which what absorbs him is not his actual death but the possibility for self-expression that the drama affords. And why should an opportunity for self-expression—so strikingly, almost farcically, inappropriate to his particular situation—tempt him so? We need but briefly remind ourselves of his condition, and the extraordinary vulnerabilities common to it, to guess that the explanation for his response lies in what he believes is being promised him in return for the cooperation he so wholeheartedly supplies. What can this promise be but that self-expression, given free reign in this exceptional enterprise, will produce for him the dramatic representation of some uniqueness, some singularity of self with which life has seemingly so far failed to provide him, and of which his natural—unself-engineered—death threatens to rob him? What I wish to point out here is that all this is a dream of the will—a despairing attempt to affirm the self in a form in which the self has never been and can never be. The uncertainties—and even the terrors—of death belong, as Kirillov almost discovered, to life and to our nature. Living the life of suicide a man struggles to deny this truth, and should the trapdoor spring open beneath him, he will die proclaiming his denial. But, it is a redeeming paradox of the life of suicide that it does not always—and need not—make its exit from life via the trapdoor. The despairing man can return to life—alive. Many have done so, and some have left their accounts of that treacherous passage to remind us that salvation is never wholly out of reach, even in the farthest country of despair.

5

WILL AND
WILLFULNESS
IN HYSTERIA

Early in Freud's career as a psychoanalyst, he suffered a spell
of rapture in which he boasted to Fliess that he could cure
every case of hysteria. Though he was now in his middle
years, this exuberance really belonged to his therapeutic youth,
a time when his medical past still suffused and shaped his view
of psychology. If, at this stage, the strategies of psychotherapy
seemed as specific as a scalpel, hysteria was for him, literally,
a hidden abscess bloated with the debris of sexual trauma—an
abscess that must be located, then opened to consciousness,
before the systemic symptoms of this malady would disappear.
(It is my impression that most psychoanalysts have passed
through this phase of development, although it must be admitted a few have lingered here unconscionably long.) For
Freud, at least, little time passed before he inflicted such drain-
age on an abscess of hysteria—only to discover that his patient
shared neither his enthusiasm nor his optimism. In fact, after

99

only a few weeks, she ended treatment, never to return. His account of this therapeutic disaster contains one of the most anguished statements in the literature of psychology, a *cri de coeur* which must have helped him to leave his medical youth behind.

(She) had listened to me without any of her usual contradictions. She seemed to be moved; she said good-bye to me very warmly, with the heartiest wishes for the New Year, and—came no more. . . . I knew (she) would not come back again. Her breaking off so unexpectedly, just when my hopes of a successful termination of the treatment were at their highest, and her thus bringing those hopes to nothing—this was an unmistakable act of vengeance on her part. Her purpose of self-injury also profited by this action. No one who, like me, conjures up the most evil of those half-tamed demons that inhabit the human breast, and seeks to wrestle with them, can expect to come through the struggle unscathed. Might I perhaps have kept the girl under my treatment if I myself had acted a part, if I had exaggerated the importance to me of her staying on, and had shown a warm personal interest in her—a course which, even after allowing for my position as her physician, would have been tantamount to providing her with a substitute for the affection she longed for? I do not know. Since in every case a portion of the factors that are encountered under the form of resistance remains unknown, I have always avoided acting a part, and have contented myself with practising the humbler arts of psychology. In spite of every theoretical interest and of every endeavour to be of assistance as a physician, I keep the fact in mind that there must be some limits set to the extent to which psychological influence may be used, and I respect as one of these limits the patient's own *will and understanding* [italics mine].[1]

Within this outcry can be discerned the frantic flailings of spirit that would declare to the world the pain this perverse creature had inflicted on him and, at the same time, give rational form to his outrage. It is despair that demands that she be charged with both the cunning to know that his "hopes . . .

[1] Sigmund Freud, "Fragment of a Case of Hysteria" (1905), *Collected Papers* (New York: Basic Books, 1959), Vol. III, pp. 131-132.

were at their highest," as well as the meanness to shatter these hopes. Equally understandable is the simultaneous conviction, barely skirting the edges of self-pity and self-aggrandizement, that such catastrophes must be the penalty for ventures as heroic as his. At this point his pain subsides, the rhetorical scale diminishes, and he turns to reason for consolation and even instruction, seeking an order and detachment that so far have eluded him. As if he had now forgotten his violent description of her impact on him, he wonders in his new mood if he might not have deliberately "exaggerated" to her the importance of remaining in treatment. But, he could not countenance such pretense on his part. Almost safely past the claims of indignation, he can now hope, in the teeth of what has just occurred, that he has always contented himself with "practising the humbler arts of psychology." He can acknowledge that there are limits to psychological influence. It is precisely at this point that he comes to a glimmering of the truth about his experience with Dora: "I respect as one of these limits [of psychological influence] the patient's own *will and understanding.*" In other words, regardless of the inventiveness and accuracy with which he and Dora have traced the origins and meanings of her disorder, there is a force in her that says "no" to this mutual creation. To this force he gave the name allotted to it by history, namely, will. At the same time, he simultaneously, and even paradoxically, ruled this traditional category out of bounds. But did this mean that henceforth the will, as it had been understood by the ages, was to be excluded from his psychological considerations? Not entirely. In his postscript to the case of Dora, his anguish had subsided to the extent that he could more calmly consider his therapeutic failure:

I have been obliged to speak of transference, for it is only by means of this factor that I can elucidate the peculiarities of Dora's analysis. Its great merit, namely, the unusual clarity which makes it seem so suitable as a first introductory publication, is closely bound up with its great defect, which led to its being broken off prematurely. I did not succeed in mastering the transference in good time. . . . In this way the transference took me unaware, and, because of the unknown quantity in me which reminded Dora of Herr K., she took her revenge on me as she wanted to take her revenge on him. . . . If cruel impulses and revengeful motives, which have already been used in the patient's ordinary life for maintaining her symptoms, become transferred on to the physician during treatment, before he has had time to detach them from himself by tracing them back to their sources, then it is not to be wondered at if the patient's condition is unaffected by his therapeutic efforts.[2]

In other words, he no longer recognizes the "limits . . . to which psychological influence may be used"—i.e., will and understanding—and is instead elaborating his theories of transference, which were to prove so significant for therapy. However, "tracing . . . cruel impulses and revengeful motives . . . back to their sources" is not quite the same at considering the psychology of will itself. In fact, it could be said that Freud in his postscript chose to limit himself to a fragment of the problem of will: its motivations. And, what he thought these motivations to be is clearly stated in the same postscript:

I was further anxious to show that sexuality . . . provides the motive power for every single symptom, and for every single manifestation of a symptom. The symptoms of the disease are nothing else than *the patient's sexual activity*.[3]

Thus, as was so often the case with Freud, the problem of will was equated with the motive of sexuality. For every act, a variety of motives can be adduced—anxiety, sex, ambition, prestige, aggression, and so on, but even if we grant their validity as motives, their temporal priority cannot automatically endow them with ontological, nor psychological, superi-

[2] *Ibid.*, pp. 141–144.
[3] *Ibid.*, p. 137.

ority to the act itself. A motive cannot explain an act; the act must ultimately be judged on its own terms. Though we must be grateful for the second glance that permitted Freud to develop his theories of transference, I should like to suggest that his first impassioned outcry caught more of the truth about hysteria.

My thesis is that hysteria is a particular disorder of will whose principal expression is willfulness. By willfulness, I do not mean mere intention or determination, which are older definitions of the term. I am using here *Webster's* more contemporary definition, namely "governed by will, without yielding to reason; obstinate; perverse; stubborn; as a willful man or horse." This definition suggests that, in willfulness, the life of the will becomes distended, overweening, and obtrusive at the same time that its movements become increasingly separate, sovereign, and distinct from other aspects of spirit. And, with distention of will that is relatively unrelieved, intellect is bound to suffer. I mean, of course, intellect in the large sense, including not only will's usual adversary, which is reason, but also imagination, humor, discretion, and judgment. In willfulness, then, will pursues its own tyrannical course with reckless disdain for what we usually mean by content, unless that content be will itself.

In willfulness, the will does the work of the imagination. Though rather quaint and crude, no better example of this situation exists than that bizarre occasion called hypnosis, in which hysteric-as-hypnotist barters with hypnotist-as-hysteric, making it impossible to say at any given moment who is Trilby. It could be argued that hypnosis is one of hysteria's necessary and characteristic inventions. Even the persistence of its early nineteenth-century trappings (though the cloak and flowing tie have been replaced by a business suit) testifies to the intransigent, mindless quality of hysteria's inventiveness, which stays so indifferent to historical context. So little, really, has the form of hypnosis changed, that it would seem to be lifted bodily from the pages of a Gothic novel of the period. Let us remember that at the same time Mesmer was discovering Nature's magnetic forces within himself, Shelley was augmenting his own powers by merging with the west wind. "Be thou, spirit fierce, my spirit!" he cried. "Be thou me, impetuous one!"[4] The prime quality of that romantic movement, according to Allen Tate, was "the momentary illusion of individual power." "The romantic," wrote Tate, "ranged over nature in the effort to impose his volitional ego as an absolute on the world."[5]

The illusions of absolute power and absolute compliance that occupy hypnosis are necessarily momentary and fragile, quickly dispelled by the intrusions of life or psychotherapy, which is why they seem reserved largely for hypnosis, and why hypnosis itself seems so unlike anything else in life. To maintain these illusions requires the unflagging will of both parties, "will" here meaning the "willful suspension of disbelief." The first events of hypnosis, which usually consist of the hypnotist's exploitation of such items as gravity, muscular fatigue, and inertia, are seldom questioned by the subject, but are arbitrarily attributed to the hypnotist's powers. And, a "good" hypnotist will initially resist, just as much as his subject, any rational formulation of these events, since his dramatic or hypnotic effectiveness hinges on his *own* belief in his powers. Qualities suggesting the "merely human," such as self-consciousness, doubt, and humor, in either the hypnotist or the subject, are inimical to the pact of hypnosis, which must be irrational and romantic to succeed. In Melville's sense, each participant should be a Confidence Man—i.e., a man who has

[4] Percy Bysshe Shelley, "Ode to the West Wind," *Poets of the English Language* (New York: The Viking Press, 1950), Vol. IV, p. 332.
[5] Allen Tate, "Three Types of Poetry," *On the Limits of Poetry* (New York: The Swallow Press & William Morris, 1948), pp. 100–101.

confidence. It is understandable why, in terms of his development, hypnosis is apt to be an absorption of the youthful psychiatrist, embraced most passionately during the period when his skills are least formed. Hypnosis becomes one willful way of overriding the despair of the young psychiatrist, not yet qualified by age or humanity to give counsel. At this stage in life, the romanticism of science urges him to dip into Nature for the verification of his own powers. Once the hypnotist begins to lose his belief, it will not be long before the spectacle strikes him as comic, for—retrospectively, at least—outbursts of will are apt to appear more comic than pathetic, because of the unadorned combination of presumption and ignorance.

Once having been isolated as willfulness, the will can no longer step outside itself, so that its inventiveness must be within its own terms. While willfulness may seize other categories, under its dominion these categories lose their original substance, serving only as illusions of themselves. It has been said that hysteria and hypnosis have been used to prove every possible psychological theory, including psychoanalysis. But, of course, under the sway of the two parent illusions of hypnosis—absolute power and absolute compliance—what is apt to be proved is the power of hypnosis, rather than any particular theory of psychopathology. Although the theories contrived may be wildly different in form, they are invariably coercive in nature, describing how the will of the child is assaulted by the will of the parents. Thus, the will invents in its own image. It may be recalled that Freud at first took the tales of early seduction of his hysterical patients quite literally, only to discover that these episodes were more in the realm of fantasy. Eventually, he managed to reconcile this error with his previous theories about sexuality. But, what he failed to note was that, in either case, the will had contrived its own willful theory. No phase of existence is so easily appropriated to the needs of the will as sexuality. But both erotic adventures that are invented, and those that are lived, must be read allegorically as episodes in willfulness, so that form will not be mistaken for content, or expression for cause. It is precisely this confusion that has led to several errors about hysteria that still persist today, even though our therapeutic experience refutes them. Because the hysteric is so absorbed with sexual drama, in fact and in fantasy, and because he brings this form of willfulness almost immediately into the therapeutic situation, it has been assumed that such sexual freedom entitled hysteria to a top position in the libidinal hierarchy. The fact of the matter, as most therapists will agree, is that hysteria deserves no such rank, remaining one of the most incorrigible states taxing the therapist. Another common assumption, equally mistaken, was the belief that with sexual emancipation, hysteria would disappear. In point of fact, sexual emancipation, and the spread of physiological and anatomical knowledge, have merely diminished the cruder conversion manifestations. It was often the case that the hysteric, in stress, might in a sense exert the same absolute dominion over his own body that he exerted over others. What he would not move was paralyzed; what he would not hear deafened him; what he would not see blinded him. The hysteric's peremptory dealings with his own body would resemble the changes wrought by the hypnotist on the person of his subject; and, in both cases, the signals for these impositions could be as arbitrary as the numbers from one to ten.

Before sexual emancipation, willfulness in sex was restricted to whether the person would or would not. With emancipation, willfulness shifted from the fact of participation to an absorption with the details of the sexual act itself. It is a larger arena we have built for the hysteric, and the rules are more complicated, now that sexual performance has been atomized, with each particle exploitable. When Freud called a spade a spade to Dora, giving the sexual functions their clinical appellations, he offered Dora a new range of metaphor, if her vocabulary was that of the usual woman of her class. Nor was fresh metaphor all he offered, for his theory of symbolism endowed even her ordinary expressions and activities with sexual importance. It may be asked, however, whether such exegesis constitutes emancipation, or whether, instead, the means of expression are merely extended. To put it another way, and possibly more exactly, what Freud may have achieved was a change from the method of concealment to that of disclosure, without necessarily altering the motivation.

The manner of hysteria, viewed critically from outside the experience of the beholder, will usually be described with adjectives derived more from theater than from psychology. "Dramatic" or "histrionic," used pejoratively, are the terms most commonly invoked to convey the hysteric's impact. They suggest a repertoire of personal decoration, gesture, intonation, and even vocabulary, whose flourish puts more modest or commonplace devices of expressiveness to shame and is disproportionate to the spoken or written message. If a choice can be made between the physical and psychic realms, this repertoire belongs more to the former, even though it uses psychic materials. When this dramatic insistence becomes too overpowering, whatever intellectual substance there may be is blurred for the listener, whose attention finds itself split in a manner not unlike the division in the hysteric. In such fragmentation, listening, in any honorable sense, is no longer possible. Instead, mannerisms of body and voice, formerly inconspicuous, acquire a new and crude existence, widely separated from what is said. As the beholder's attention hesitates between these two poles, the possibility of any fully imaginative response recedes: he must now choose between style and content, such choice necessarily involving his own will. Inevitably, now, he compels himself, whether in agreement or disagreement, to address himself to the hysteric's manner. Thus does it happen that will responds to will, and dialogue can be no more than illusion.

In an absolute, or dialogic, sense, in which manner and content can be separated only arbitrarily, hysterical drama may be said to be bad drama. Everyone has his own style of expression. Even the deadpan "objective" approach, in its seeming absence of style, intends to accord "scientific" or "sensible" or "unemotional" substantiation to a statement. Yet, for most people their dramatic style will have an intimate, though wavering, bearing on their thought, with sometimes one, and sometimes the other, being in the ascendancy—still without the connection being lost. However, it is quite possible for very little to be said extravagantly well, in which case the listener may be persuaded that he has heard more than he can later remember at a moment when the speaker's manner has faded from his recollection: "I can't remember what he said, but he had a most charming way of expressing himself." Here the important word, of course, is "himself," for when the disproportion between manner and message is great, when manner turns so top-heavy as to be called hysterical, personal style in its self-assertiveness would enhance not the idea so much as the brilliance and charm of its author.

"Flirtatious," "coquettish," or "seductive" would describe hysterical behavior where the drama is apparently sexual. Apparently—because were it clearly sexual, the adjectives would no longer apply. The seducer suggests his availability without quite acknowledging his intention. Thus, his manner will consist of persuasive or coercive nudgings, hardly overt enough for an overture, for extorting sexual commitment. Although these stratagems may be unacknowledged, it would be improper to call them "unconscious." Let us say that their recognition would impose a problem in morality which might diminish the excitement of the campaign. Recognition is postponed rather than repressed. The theory that the stratagems themselves are witless manifestations of dark sexual forces—puppets whose strings are pulled by the libido—is welcomed by the hysteric because it absolves him of willful intent. He is *acted upon* by Nature, who works her will on him. So long as both wills—his and Nature's—reside within his person, there can be no defeat; victory is his, whatever the outcome. Though the defeat of his will may, in reality, have brought him to treatment, this theory offers him a way of viewing that defeat as a victory for Nature's will, an outcome not too uncommon in the speculations of the nineteenth century. Returning to seduction, once the partner commits himself sexually, the will may find another goal in fending off that commitment. The will's nimbleness in shifting goals has been aptly called "teasing," the organ prefix depending on the sex of the partner. With the idolatry of sex through sexology and psychoanalysis, opportunities for the will have increased, through the appropriation of the details of sexual union. In an age characterized to some extent by "the tyranny of the orgasm," the choice is no longer between sex or no sex; instead, the will joins itself to those particles of sexual behavior whose sum, it is hoped, will constitute the sexual act. When this particular absorption with the willful possibilities of sex occurs at the feverish beginnings of psychotherapy, it is apt to be called "positive transference," and to be mistakenly considered a good omen for cure. During this phase, before the two wills begin to oppose each other, the hysteric makes sexuality out of the therapist's science, while the therapist makes science out of sexuality. In this affair, the hysteric has the advantage, there being more sex to science than vice versa. The therapist's disadvantage, moreover, is increased by his habit—encouraged by psychoanalytic theory—of isolating the sexual function: whether his language is clinical or vernacular, he works on the brink of pornography. To serve pornography, sexuality must be torn from the larger human context and exalted into a life of its own.

What Tate has said of the romantic imagination applies equally to hysteria: "It has no insight into the total meanings of actual moral situations; it is concerned with fictitious alternatives to them, because they invariably mean frustration of the will."[6] If, at this precise moment in my writing, I fall into conflict about how best to develop the hysteric's incapacity for conflict; if now there seem several possible ways, all with their privileges and limitations, yet none leading in a conclusive direction; I may suddenly discover myself moving briskly away from my chair, possessed by the almost physical necessity to walk to the drugstore, where I shall case the paperback collection and purchase a second toothbrush. If I am harsher with myself than is my custom, I will wonder briefly what I am doing on this expedition, and my answers will probably have to do with fresh air and exercise. Should I be so foolish as to assure myself that this little trip allows me to think my way out of a writing dilemma, I shall have to confess that there have been no thoughts: only a trip and a purchase—a compulsive voyage, a quickly achieved, though irrelevant, goal, and, finally, a return to this same chair, to begin again. The example is a deliberately trivial instance of my will inventing a fictitious alternative for me at a time when conflict would be more suitable. Obviously, many activities that enjoy the name of distraction are actually the fictitious alternatives the will devises for sidestepping possible moral conflict. To a great extent, the emotionality of hysteria, ranging from rage to tears, can be understood as the fictitious alternative to real conflict. And, in hysteria, much of what is called by such names as "impulsivity" or "acting out" are more serious, even catastrophic, adventures invented by the will, alcohol being one of its most faithful accomplices in

[6] *Ibid.*, p. 102.

these escapades: it performs the double service of inflating the will at the same time as it dulls discrimination.

As Tate has suggested, a moral situation must involve "frustration of the will," and a fictitious alternative to this frustration can be, in hysteria, a new and feverish exertion of will. The advantage of this willful exertion is the illusion of wholeness, forcibly grasped rather than gained or granted. Unlike the first realm of will, not only is there no joined totality of the privileges of mind and body, but there is a serious diminution of ordinary capacities, although this may not be immediately apparent. What we are likely to experience in this state is not the freedom of the first realm, but rather the exhilaration that we are, at last and again, doing what we want to do. In such excitement, the self *is* the will, but it is no longer that shadowy, elusive creature, flickering over the surface of consciousness, that we traditionally call the self. Thanks to the work of the will, the self emerges whole into the bright light of the world: suddenly it has acquired shape and dimension and substance: it has been concretized by the will. But the faint resemblance that this imposing apparition bears to the true nature of the self, testifies both to the formidable powers of the will, as well as to the urgency of the need we all share to experience wholeness. When wholeness eludes us in its proper setting—in dialogue—so vital is it to our lives that we turn wildly to will, ready to grasp at any illusion of wholeness, however mindless or grotesque. Caught in this illusion, and delirious with well-being, we are convinced of the extraordinary keenness and clarity of our intellect. In point of fact, no state of mind so deadens, and injures, our faculties as our belief in this illusion of wholeness. The more dependent a person becomes on this illusion, the less he is able to experience true wholeness in dialogue, and at the point where he is no longer capable of dialogue, he can be said to be *addicted* to his will.

The absence of "insight into the total meanings of actual moral situations" should not be understood merely psychologically. It is not only that possible frustration of will serves as a motive for blinking actual conflict as it arises in life. More important, will's solitary and inflated sovereignty as willfulness actively opposes the acquisition of precisely those intellectual faculties with which we perceive the "total meanings of actual moral situations." For the severely hysterical person, there has been a cumulative failure in learning over the years as he pitted his will against the will of his parent and teacher. Whether in compliance or opposition, with charm or with rancor, he could surrender himself neither to his teacher nor to his subject matter. The open admission of ignorance contained in the phrase "I don't know" is the essential precondition for learning. But, for the hysteric, "I don't know," except when used as strategy, means a defeat of will. As the gaps in learning accumulate, "I don't know" is replaced by a manner of knowingness, which is an assortment of gestures, physical and verbal, implying not merely understanding, but also the possession of far more knowledge than can be expressed in words. The hysteric considers his gaps in learning more shameful than sexual aberration and artfully hides them from the world, thus insuring their perfect isolation from the knowledge that might repair them. What was trouble with addition and subtraction in the second grade, now causes the hysteric to keep his hands hidden as he counts on his fingers. But, more ominous than arithmetical insufficiency, is the probability that his failure with numbers is closely related to his present clumsiness in logic as it pertains to himself and to the world about him. What used to be his original problem with grammar in the third grade, now exists as an impoverishment of language rendering him invulnerable to those syntactical discriminations which we call by such names as humor, irony, ambiguity, and paradox. Since we are all, to some extent, the language we speak, we cannot be surprised when an hysteric whom we have recently studied announces soberly, after reading the first chapter of *Huckleberry Finn*, that it is a sad story about an adopted child, neglected and intimidated by his foster parent. Such a reading is only in part an instance of a willful person discovering willfulness in a story where there is none: it also demonstrates his utter dependence, in making such a discovery, on his willful indifference to language itself. Though willfulness would seem accessible to psychotherapy, the hysteric's intellectual failure which has accumulated over the years will hardly respond to motive analysis or insight or even to relation therapy, although these may constitute a beginning for learning those discriminations that belong to the world of intelligence. When it is understood that hysteria consists of a double failure in the realms of will and intelligence, it is no longer mysterious that its treatment is so arduous and time-consuming. Nor is it mysterious why such treatment, ideally, should combine psychotherapy and education in the best sense of both disciplines.

If ethical considerations lie beyond the capacities of hysteria, can any generalization be made about the nature of hysterical discourse? By and large, the hysteric's way of addressing and perceiving his fellows and the world about him can be said to be aesthetic. It should be quickly noted, however, that the aestheticism of hysteria, since it is relatively uninformed by imagination and intelligence, is not of the honorable order that we often associate with the term. Moreover, the aestheticism of hysteria, being deprived of real subject matter, turns about the self, even about the body, of the hysteric. The question "What do I say and do?" becomes "How do I look when I say and do?" And, not merely "How do I look?" but "How do you look?" As my friend talks to me I may be on the verge of a critical statement about what he has said, but because my attention has wandered and my intellectual powers are stunted for the moment, I simply cannot achieve the formulation I desire. At this instant, I am struck by the fact that he is not as interesting-looking as I had thought, nor for that matter has his way of expressing himself been particularly felicitous. Let me add that I could have been on the verge of an admiring statement, which eluded me, and at the same instant I could have been struck by how well he looked and how well he spoke. Both examples involve my being reduced to aesthetic comment. The aestheticism of hysteria concerns itself with many variations on two questions: "Am I pretty?" (or "Am I manly?") and "Am I bright?" Both questions may be asked separately, sequentially, or simultaneously. In combination, they may amount to the question, "Am I interesting?" or "Do you like me?" Although these questions may be asked affirmatively when mutual endorsement is enthusiastic, when disenchantment comes, they will most probably be phrased, "You think me stupid. Or ugly. Or dull." Or, with more discouragement, "I'm a fool, a mess. How could anyone like me?" Psychoanalysis, with its theories of motivation, will extend, if not enrich, the vocabulary of the hysteric, for this aestheticism can subvert any of the categories of characterology. "Aren't you being hostile?" or "I am put off by your tone." In a sense the hysteric welcomes the motive-analysis of psychoanalysis, both as a criticism of his style, and as an opportunity to improve his manner.

Because the willful, and aesthetic, nature of hysteria has not been understood, many psychologists, including Freud, have mistakenly believed hysteria to be an almost exclusively female disorder. In fact, convinced that hysteria biologically belonged to women, they have usually located male hysteria in those varieties of homosexuality in which "femaleness" is mimicked, if not parodied. However, according to the formulation I have described in this chapter, hysteria would belong

equally to men, except that the style of discourse would
revolve around the question, "Am I manly?" An example of
male hysteria would be the enforced masculinity of Heming-
way, in his person and, to some degree, in his writing.

Such aestheticism is characteristic of those hysterical suicidal
gestures whose self-mutilations serve death only accidentally.
These gestures resemble conversion symptoms in that the
hysteric works his will on his own body. But, unlike the
conversion symptom in which the function of the body is impaired, in the suicidal attempt the intactness of the body is dis-
figured. The gesture is an aesthetic rather than an ethical comment: despairing and bitter, it mocks the body that has failed
its owner's romantic will. To the question, "Am I pretty?",
the gesture cries, "So be it! I *am* ugly!" or "If you think me
ugly, I'll *be* ugly!" In an antiaesthetic way, ugliness, rather
than death, would seem to be the object. And, this same ugliness may spread, in its own perverse fashion, over the entire
scene, affecting decor, dress, gesture, and even relationship: all
may become as disheveled as the hysteric requires.

Philosophically, the distinction between will and intellect is
an ideal one—an abstraction that, although useful in dissecting
the human spirit, has, like other abstractions, done some disservice to the potentialities for totality in existence. And psychologically, if I attempt to describe the role of will in an
unself-conscious activity, I cannot help but fragment that
activity into psychic and physical aspects whose sum bears
little resemblance to the original totality of the experience. In
our most interesting moments—dialogic moments, if you will—
will is unconscious and can only willfully be pried loose from
the rest of life. It is when will becomes conscious that it exists
separately, can be experienced separately, and can be discussed
separately. As I indicated earlier, will as willfulness may not
be acknowledged by the hysteric, but this does not mean that
it is repressed or unconscious: awareness is merely postponed.

Will as willfulness belongs to consciousness and, in varying degree, is an inescapable portion of our lives.

Subjectively, willfulness is experienced in a manner that reveals its kinship with the body. At the moment when will is preponderant, it is felt almost physically as a lunging of the body, a fact that may explain why Schopenhauer describes the body as the objectification of the will. Through will, consciousness of the physical self becomes as absorbing as physical pain. An unremitting pain, such as toothache, lands one squarely on the anterior side of the body-mind dualism: one *is* a body. One *is* mortal, and since, by definition, mortality is crumbling, its claims are imperious. In pain one observes the drama of his failing body, all thought centered on the aching part. On the other hand, when will is ascendant, no spectator-self observes the rush of the will; at the most, one may be aware of a breathless thrusting of self that may literally cause the body to lean forward. Will is now felt as personal weight with its own momentum, expressing itself in such questions as, "Do you know what I mean?" or "Do you follow me?" With these questions, one reveals his awareness that the thought, or prethought, which lurched awkwardly through conversation, was fortified not so much by imagination as by personal emphasis, be it of body, pitch, or language. Like an idea that becomes too old too fast, its propulsive gait could not be healed, only affirmed. In willfulness, one is like a man who has lost his chance to tell his anecdote to the assembled party and now waits to seize the next opportunity. People seem to go on talking in what could be a foreign language. They look interested, knowing. They even seem to share in the allotted space in the air about them, much like a page of printed dialogue, indented every line or so, and seen for its typographical arrangement rather than for its meaning. Finally, there is or is not a pause, and he says, "This has been reminding me of . . .", and on with the story. The pathetic attempt to assert a relevance to his story stems from an awareness that will has dulled his responsiveness, isolating him from all that has gone before, yet still demanding to be heard.

This feverish figure, endlessly assaulting the company, seeking to wrench the moment to some pretense of dialogue, is the image of the eternal stranger: that condition of man in which he is forever separated from his fellows, unknown and unaddressed. It is the figure of man's separated will posing as his total self. Though always a stranger to those he moves among, this figure is no stranger to our imagination. Who is he but ourselves—you and I and everyman—as we have been over and over in the past and shall be again? This condition of willfulness, which at once drives us to grasp for wholeness and prevents our attainment of it, is no rare disease. Even by its harsher, clinical term, hysteria, it is, in varying degree, the lot of each of us. The temptations of will beset us all, because they belong inevitably to the human condition. That being the case, I should like to conclude with a word or two in defense of hysteria, but I am afraid that note of uplift is denied me. The most impressive claim made on behalf of hysteria is that the willful gestures characterizing it are often the necessary opening moves we make in overcoming the fear, despair, doubt, timidity, lethargy, or excessive rationality that may come upon us at the outset of any new venture and render our indispensable commitment impossible. This claim asserts that hysteria is a prelude to passion. I would maintain that, far from being a prelude or a preparation, hysteria is passion's deadly adversary; hysteria loathes passion as a potential usurper of its usurped domain. With similar shrewdness it abhors wit, discrimination, imagination, humor, and judgment—all those aspects of intelligence whose injury and impairment are its goal and result. It is true that we must live with hysteria, but we need not, I think, honor it. In fact, if we give it its rightful identification as the sworn enemy of our capacity to be fully human, we may give ourselves a crucial advantage in the struggle we must constantly engage in to transcend it.

6

FACES OF ENVY

Unlike most words having to do with the human condition, the definitions of envy I have seen are remarkably similar. Unlike other moral terms in the West, whose meanings shift with the temper of the times, the etymology of envy has stayed unusually constant. Envy had the same meaning for Plato that it had for Sullivan. When Horace wrote in the first century that "Sicilian tyrants never invented a greater torment than envy," he was concerned with the sheer and ubiquitous "pain of mind," expressed by Onasander, that caused Richard Sheridan to observe, in the eighteenth century, that "there is not a passion so strongly rooted in the human heart as envy." Dante devised for envy, which he counted as one of the seven deadly sins, a torment chillingly apt: in his Inferno the eyelids of the envious were sewn together. Such punishment would have suited Onasander, who wrote in A.D. 49 that "envy is a pain of mind that successful men cause their neighbors." More recently, it might have seemed equally fitting to Max Beerbohm when he suggested that "the dullard's envy of brilliant men is always assuaged by the suspicion that they will come to a bad end."

Stressing its subjective nature, the usual definition of envy is "chagrin or discontent at the excellence or good fortune of another." Since such feelings are rarely suffered in silence, some definitions include an objective expression of ill-will, such as disparagement of the envied one (although disparagement is only one of the manifest paths envy may take). For more than two thousand years, this is the meaning envy has borne. My scholarship has perhaps been too casual, but I find it very odd that it is so difficult to discover a systematic treatment for so common and so painful a human experience as envy, whether one looks in the theological, philosophical, or psychological literature. References are scanty and fleeting, and often epigrammatic, suggesting that envy's origins in human history and its manifestations in human sensibility and conduct are not easily discoverable. My guess is that envy, by its very nature, is obstinate in its opposition to investigation.

The protean character of envy and its talent for disguise account, I believe, for the infrequency of studies on the subject. Because of the variety of forms it may take, it is often simply impossible to recognize. This is true, not only for the observer, who by definition must be more gullible about such a subjective state as envy, but also for the envious one himself, whose rational powers may lend almost unholy assistance to the need for self-deception. Therefore, anecdotal examples of envy are usually crude. For instance, I remember with some clarity the first time I heard Harry Stack Sullivan lecture. His subject matter escapes me now as it escaped me then, but how well I recall him fussing with the recording apparatus. As I later explained to a friend, I was appalled that such a respected figure in our profession could so nakedly address himself to posterity. Wanting, of course, to give my friend a wholly objective picture of the occasion, I went on to depict Sullivan's affectations of manner and phraseology, always careful to preface each objective statement with some generous remark such as: "Don't think me envious, because I know this man to be a genius in the field of psychiatry. So it is doubly unfortunate, and so on." The example is as crude as my envy was strong. Inasmuch as envy rendered me impervious to the content of his lecture, the object of my disparagement, it will be noted, was his personal style. What I clearly observed in that style was his egotism, his infatuation with self, his dramatic need to impress that self on both posterity and on his more immediate audience. In brief, I detested his self-assertion, which is not an uncommon focus when envy takes the form of disparagement. But what of my own self-assertion? Certainly to my friend, I dissembled the degree to which I was at a loss at this particular lecture and concealed the misery and stupidity fostered by my envy, which prevented me from giving him any idea of what Sullivan had said. Instead I asserted myself brashly and authoritatively, if unhappily, representing a confidence in my own abilities that was, at that moment, as necessary as it was undeserved.

Two authors have thought self-assertion to be so crucial in envy that they might have punished the envious in the Inferno by sewing together their lips, instead of their eyelids. Kierkegaard, contrasting envy and admiration, wrote that envy was unhappy self-assertion, while admiration was happy self-surrender. And Alfred Adler, speaking of aggressive children, wrote that "when the desire for self-assertion becomes extraordinarily intense, it will always involve an element of envy." On a prescriptive basis, it would seem that self-assertion was the best way of diminishing another's importance, while at the same time redressing one's own limitations. But, in the more devious forms of envy, self-assertion may not be so apparent, even though it is implicit. Take an example of what could be called "self-assertion by proxy." Using an instance from his own day, Thomas Hobbes wrote that "the praise of ancient authors proceeds not from the reverence of the dead, but from . . . envy of the living." Or, to use our own idiom, we might say to a colleague, more envied than admired, "I thought your paper excellent. Incidentally, didn't you get your central idea from a letter Freud wrote to Ferenczi on his fiftieth birthday?" Seemingly, with such a disheartening compliment, we merely refer to Freud's priority and trust that our demeanor is properly self-effacing. On the other hand, if our colleague is one of those suspicious, thin-skinned fellows, he might very well think we were making a tiny claim for our scholarship in psychoanalytic matters, while withholding any real praise for his own effort. Indeed, one of envy's favorite stratagems is the attempt to provoke envy in the envied one —in this case, either for Freud's priority and prestige, or for our encyclopedic acquaintance with the field, or for both. There is something about the insistent nature of envy's self-assertion that makes it almost impossible to down. And, it is just as hard for the envier to admit his self-assertion as it is to admit envy itself.

Suppose, still envious, we had chosen to chasten our colleague in this manner: "I don't remember when I've been so moved, so impressed. You are simply marvelous on this subject. You have an absolute genius for throwing a new light on difficult questions." As an actor with many faces, envy may try to pass itself off as its exact opposite—namely, admiration. Yet, when envy is the motive, admiration loses its tie both to affection and to the occasion, becoming wholly subject to the will. Unlike true admiration, which, because it is free of conscious will always has the option of silence, envy's imitation of admiration clamors for public acknowledgment; the more stinging his envy, the more ardently must the envious one dramatize himself as an admirer whose passion overshadows and shames the more reticent responses of others. However, since it is as futile to will admiration as it is to will affection, this attempt at praise, inevitably self-assertive, turns excessive, inappropriate, and even irrelevant. Whereas true admiration keeps its distance, respecting the discrepancy between the admirer and the admired one, envy's assault upon its object with a barrage of compliments serves not only its need to assert itself in the costume of admiration, but also the lust of the envier to possess the very quality that initially incited his envy.

To some extent envy is always a divisive experience, alienating us, not only from our fellows, but also from our own rational powers. We tend to forget that praise, just as much as criticism, may become an *ad hominem* venture when envy divorces us from our subject matter. If envy can move us to disparage our colleague's life rather than his subject, so can it move us to exalt his life at the expense of his subject. We tend to assume, mistakenly, that praise of another's character is the highest compliment we can offer him, overlooking how conveniently we may employ such inevitably general and abstract expressions of approval in an effort to avoid making a direct and concrete response to what he has said or done or produced, this being certainly the most relevant and satisfying praise for the subject himself. Undiscriminating praise may, in fact, have a harsher effect on the envied one than criticism: it may arouse his own envy toward the exalted image we impose on him and, in his awareness of the immense disparity between it and his own image of himself, remind him ever more sharply of his limitations.

The least differentiated, and perhaps most childish, shape which envy may assume is that of greed. By ordinary greed I mean merely the craving to possess the world's goods, whether food, drink, flattery, sex, parents, money, or psychoanalysis. In its materialistic and undiscriminating fashion, greed will take little notice of the manner or distinction that allowed their owner to acquire these goods. Greed is not necessarily restricted to those objects I do not have: I can be just as greedy for those goods which I already have in abundance. On the other hand, if I envy you, I begrudge you some quality or qualities of being which I do not possess: your wisdom, your dignity, your courage, your humility. What characterizes such virtues is that, although I may perceive and admire—or envy—them in you, your possession of them lies outside your self-consciousness; they may become a matter of concern to you only insofar as you lack them, or when you, in turn, recognize them in others. Most accomplishments and some virtues do not have this paradoxical nature. Skill or tact or a capacity for honesty, for example, may be pursued directly; to acknowledge and enjoy possession of them does not contradict their nature. But, only the fool proclaims his wisdom, only the proud man, his humility, only the coward, his courage. Not only do these virtues make a liar of the man who claims them, they forever evade any effort to achieve them. I may seek knowledge; I may not seek to be wise. Sharing an essential freedom from self-concern (which also characterizes the capacity for admiration), such virtues are not accomplishments and cannot be learned. They must be deserved, but their possession is a matter of grace, and is given only to him who denies it. If I observe a skill of yours, or some virtue to which imitation *is* appropriate, admiration may move me to emulate you, to work for such skill, to practice that virtue myself. But, when I perceive in you a quality of being such as I have described, my admiration may not move in the direction of emulation: I cannot imitate or learn from you; the attainment of such qualities is as removed from will of the second realm as their possession must be from self-knowledge. I may merely behold your virtue—and acknowledge my own inferiority. This is the most generous, and the most difficult, gesture admiration is called on to make. If my generosity fails, my response turns envious. Posing as greed, my envy will blink the virtues that aroused it and fasten instead on some material possession that has perhaps come to you by virtue of your distinction. Whether I now ridicule or covet this possession is not so important as the seeming advantage that I gain by reducing my envy to greed and you to your possession. There is some irony in the circumstance that we have an entire advertising industry deliberately exploiting envy-qua-greed by asserting the proposition that a man is what he owns. The irony is compounded when we remember that we have a sociology of class dedicated to precisely the same proposition. So long as I believe that you are your possessions and that my motive is greed, I can avoid any acknowledgment of the essential inequality between us. However, unless I am especially talented at self-deception, this advantage will reveal itself as illusory; certainly, if I manage to acquire your goods and to satisfy what I imagine to be my greed, the poor comfort this affords me will hasten the exposure of my real motive.

Unlike greed and jealousy, with which it is often confused, envy arises from a person's apprehension of another's superiority, and his consequent critical evaluation of himself. Indeed, it is just this aspect of envy that inspires the envier's zeal and inventiveness in denying it. Greed affords little pleasure, jealousy only pain. However, neither requires one to acknowledge a deficiency of quality in himself. Greed admits one's lack of some material object whose acquisition depends not at all on his worthiness of it, but simply on his luck or will in attaining it. Jealousy acknowledges a threat (which may or may not be real)—the possible loss of some possession greatly valued, usually someone's love. Jealousy does not depend, however, on knowledge of the agent of the threat, but merely on knowledge, or suspicion, that a rival exists. If the rival is known, he may invoke envy as well as jealousy in the threatened person. When both emotions are present, they almost inevitably lose their separate identities in the abundance and commotion of feeling; indeed, they often connive at their confusion with one another, each gaining some advantage from concealment and sharing, as they do, fear, resentment, and blindness toward the rival, who ceases to be known in any personal, detached way, becoming merely his effect upon the jealous-envious sufferer. (This reduction of another person is both an aim and an effect of envy and jealousy, alike.) However, despite their kinship, their similarities, their attraction for each other, their eagerness to dress up in one another's clothes, jealousy and envy are, in fact, both different and separate, notwithstanding the reluctance of committed victims, as well as disinterested students, to concern themselves with a distinction. Jealousy is a monothematic, romantic drama involving three characters, one of whom—the jealous person—doubles variously as author, director, stage-manager, critic, and audience, according to the needs of each plot. Despite the anguished subjectivity of most of the dialogue, the issues of the conflict—loss and gain—are external to character and even to self-esteem (what causes humiliation and the fall of self-esteem in the jealous person is not the wound of his loss, but his jealousy itself), and the three starring figures are required to sacrifice a large measure of individuality to the ritual of their roles. Envy, by contrast, displays itself dramatically only in disguise, and involves two instead of three people, one of whom, by virtue of his self-assertion, is clearly the star; in fact, the scene does not require the actual presence of the other at all (although if it is played in his company he must be given a line or two for the sake of form). While the envied one obviously cannot be anonymous, as the rival in jealousy can be, he rarely represents any external threat to the person who envies him, so that the central conflict in envy is internal and subjective to the envier. Envy is essentially static rather than dramatic; it has very little movement and no dramatic continuity of its own; and, it shapes its expression to conditions rather than plot. Jealousy, on the other hand, insists on a relentless continuity; it eats conditions and spews out plot; obsessively, it gathers more and more of the world onto its stage, urging the drama onward toward its feared and assured doom.

Where jealousy has a real cause, and the loss is either imminent or actual, the jealous person is enraged, both at his beloved and at his rival, and craves, or is even greedy for, what has been, or is about to be, taken away. However, unless envy has already entered the picture on its own, the jealous loser is not envious, for he infers no superiority in the winner from the fact of his success. It has always been one of the more mysterious aspects of jealousy that, not only is it independent of envy, but that, often, the less respect—or potential envy— the jealous one feels for his rival, the more he is tortured by his jealousy. This oddity may be traceable in part to the unpredictable nature of love, which, unlike other desirable things we are told life has in store for the deserving, refuses to be earned, discriminates arbitrarily and according to a private standard, and always precedes rather than rewards worthiness. Although jealousy does not provoke envy, envy can easily stimulate jealousy in a susceptible host. And, it sometimes happens that envy initially authors the three-cornered drama of jealousy when, out of his envious lust to dispossess and his envious spite to torment his tormenter, the self-appointed rival calculatedly performs the gestures that set the play in motion.

Because of its specific and acutely painful nature and its addiction to home-made theatricals, jealousy is more readily identifiable than its stealthier sister, envy, and has consequently attracted more attention from both experts and amateurs. It may, as a result, be better understood; it has undoubtedly achieved a more imposing reputation. When Sullivan says, "jealousy is much more poignant and devastating than envy," I am inclined to agree, insofar as jealousy, which tends toward greater and greater concentration, sucking all things into itself, is thus experienced. Envy, which tends toward diffusion, hiding and effacing itself behind all things, escapes identification and confounds experience. I suspect that envy, because of its talent for disguise, may promote greater mischief, and I am convinced that the envious man is miserable, even though what he knowingly feels is not envy but perplexing pain.

For reasons of space and competence, I shall make only a few general remarks about the beginnings of envy in childhood. In one way or another, as I have tried to indicate, envy is a limp and unhappy response to another's superiority—a response that precludes, by its very nature, such vigorous activities as rivalry, imitation, or emulation. Essentially, it asks something for nothing: by demeaning the envied one and aggrandizing the envier, envy attempts to redress inequality without the risk of intervening effort or development. In this way, envy opposes change, enforces the status quo, and is inimical to learning. Being a painfully estranging experience, envy alienates the envier from the envied one and, in this way, is inimical to what might be called mutuality, or relation. In childhood, even more than in adult life, learning and relation are—ideally, at least—reciprocal movements. Neither can flourish very long without the other. (While life begins for the infant almost wholly in relation, the intrusions of self-consciousness soon bring the other pole of this dualism into being.) Learning the most ordinary physical skills in childhood occurs only in the context of relation. On the other hand, relation between a child and his parents cannot long exist of itself: inevitably, it requires learning for its perpetuation.

Envy, in its inhibition of both relation and learning, invariably feeds on itself. Out of envy, the child may abandon the acquirement of a given skill that might repair the imbalance between him and the envied person—whether it be a parent or another child—resorting instead to some uncomfortable display of self-assertion. The more skills envy forces him to relinquish, the harsher grows the discrepancy between himself and others, providing him, of course, with greater opportunity for envy.

In addition to feeding on itself, envy breeds itself. To some extent, envy in the parents will provide the conditions for envy in the child. I do not mean by this that envy itself is a learned response, although to some degree a child may learn the policy of derogation where superiority is involved, and certainly may learn that even the capacity for admiration can provoke his parents' envy. But, where envy is habitual to the parents, it is more than likely to direct itself sooner or later toward the child, and, strangely enough, to fasten on those qualities and capacities of his that the parents most admire. The child will probably at first find the invidious comparisons to which his parents' envy subjects him bewildering, arbitrary, and jolting to his own wavering experience of himself. In a house where envy is in the air, however, the child need but look, listen, and breathe, to be instructed in consolation and counterattack. If he submits to such instruction he will respond in kind to the envy that is aimed at him, by imitating its self-assertive gestures; in embracing that which is inimical to relation, he conspires with his parents to substitute a style, dramatizing and posing as relation, for relation; in imitating that which is inimical to learning he learns to substitute a style, impersonating competence and authority, for learning. *If* he accepts the conditions offered him and agrees to be instructed by the example of his elders, thus will their envy breed his own. There is always, of course, the possibility that by finding, or imagining, other teachers, he will undertake to choose in a different direction.

Since childhood is a time of vast and manifold inequalities, the opportunities for envy or admiration are myriad. If the qualities of being, mentioned earlier, are beyond the perceptual reach of the child, certainly the privileges and possessions and appearances of adulthood are not. Given his intellectual limitations at this stage in life, his apprehension, whether admiring or envious, of superiority in the adults around him will be remarkably literal, concrete, and physical, reminding us of the manifestations of envy-qua-greed. Such states as penis-envy or breast-envy, which have occupied much of the psychoanalytic literature on this subject, are of this literal variety, mistaking possession of the physical attribute for the various prerogatives of adulthood. I suspect, also, that whatever its aggregation, whatever its disguise, envy, which by nature is nourished on self-consciousness, can take root in the mind only when considerable differentiation has been achieved, making its appearance in early childhood unlikely. It is my guess, however, that because of its dependence on self-awareness and its imperious claims on the will, envy's origins, although of interest, are less crucial than its manifestations and effects. In fact, the attempt to expose and explain present envy by means of propositions concerning its earliest forms, may render a service, not to the patient who seeks relief from the oppression of his envy, but to the very envy itself. Such propositions offer the envier a double temptation. Rather than contend, painfully, with his present envious feelings, which would require acknowledgment of another's excellence and his own limitation, he may fall to scrutinizing the history of his envy, contenting his conscience with an "acknowledgment" of some ancient state of mind, possibly fictional and certainly irrelevant to his immediate discomfort. Secondly, in his absorption with historical origins, he may find it all too easy to locate a "first cause" for his envy somewhere outside himself; this established, a few simple operations of logic can lead him to a deterministic reconstruction of the whole development of envy in him, guaranteeing his escape from the responsibility with which possible freedom of choice, past and present, would burden him. It seems to me that the most pressing concern, for the patient or for ourselves, in regard to so damaging and disturbing an affliction as envy, is not so much to ponder when, or even why, it may originally come into being, as to discover it now where it is, to outwit its distractions and disguises, to measure its fear of being called by name.

7

MARTIN BUBER AND PSYCHOANALYSIS

In relation to their systems, most systematizers are like a man who builds an enormous castle and lives in a shack beside it; they do not live in their own enormous buildings. But spiritually that is a decisive objection. Spiritually speaking, a man's thought must be the building in which he lives—otherwise everything is topsy-turvy.
—SÖREN KIERKEGAARD[1]

Most psychoanalysts have probably asked themselves, at one time or another, whether they most aspired to be the "genital character" with "object relations" or the "syntaxic interperson" whose interrelationships are "consensually validated." In either case, these may be only aspirations. Perhaps many psychoanalysts, like me, have settled for a modest shanty existence beside one of these splendid constructs, hoping to share in some reflected glory by living so close to the castle. And perhaps some of them have even begun to wonder whether the castle itself—though elegant enough from an aesthetic standpoint—may not, like Kafka's castle, have a strangely crippling effect on those who try to live in it.

Although the young science of psychiatry has already built several rival castles, or competing systems, so far none of them

---

[1] *The Journals of Sören Kierkegaard*, ed. and trans. by Alexander Dru (London: Oxford University Press, 1938), p. 156.

is—to my present way of thinking—fit for human habitation. Nor, for that matter, have many of their architects claimed that these systems are a way of life. Certainly Freud went to some occasional pains to dissociate his theories from those of metaphysics or religion. And yet, for lack of any other definitions of the fully human, it is virtually impossible nowadays for the psychiatrist *not* to derive his norms and standards from his own theories—thus creating definitions of man out of his fragments of psychopathology. For example:

The final stage of [genital] character formation . . . borrows from [the preceding stages] whatever conduces to a favorable relation between the individual and his objects. From the early oral stage it takes over enterprise and energy; from the anal stage, endurance, perseverance . . . from sadistic sources, the necessary power to carry on the struggle for existence. If the development of his character has been successful, the individual is able to avoid falling into pathological exaggerations of those characteristics, whether in a positive or a negative direction.[2]

[Mature dependence] is characterized neither by a one-sided attitude of incorporation nor by an attitude of primary emotional identification. On the contrary, it is characterized by a capacity on the part of a differentiated individual for cooperative relationships with differentiated objects. So far as the appropriate biological object is concerned, the relationship, is, of course, genital; but it is a relationship involving evenly matched giving and taking between two differentiated individuals who are mutually dependent, and between whom there is no disparity of dependence.[3]

The self-dynamism is "the relatively enduring organization of processes which manifests itself in situations related to former experiences of anxiety . . ."[4]

[2] Karl Abraham, "Genital Character Formation," *Selected Papers of Karl Abraham* (London: Hogarth Press, 1942), p. 415.

[3] W. Ronald D. Fairbairn, *An Object-Relations Theory of the Personality* (New York: Basic Books, 1954), p. 145.

[4] Harry Stack Sullivan, as quoted in Patrick Mullahy, "The Theories of H. S. Sullivan," in *The Contributions of Harry Stack Sullivan,* ed. Patrick Mullahy (New York: Hermitage House, 1952), p. 39.

A person is a psychic system which, when it affects another person, enters into reciprocal reaction with another psychic system.[5]

Without examining these normative statements in detail, the reader can see why psychiatry is so often charged with being reductive. For, though the creatures described above may bear some resemblance to animals or to steam engines or robots or electronic brains, they do not sound like people. They are, in fact, constructs of theory, more humanoid than human; and, whether they are based on the libido theory or on one of the new interpersonal theories of relationships, it is just those qualities most distinctively human that seem to have been omitted. It is a matter of some irony, if one turns from psychology to one of Dostoyevsky's novels, to find that, no matter how wretched, how puerile, or how dilapidated his characters may be, they all possess more humanity than the ideal man who lives in the pages of psychiatry.

For the sake of emphasis, I am, of course, being somewhat extreme. The fact of the matter is that we psychiatrists, even more than our patients, maintain a happy inconsistency. We live much of our lives, professional and private, in Kierkegaard's shack, or, rather, we live according to that loose repository of wisdom, largely Judeo-Christian, that is known as "common sense." Insofar as we consent to be thus illogical or inconsistent, we are enabled to draw on the whole treasury of history for our knowledge of what is human. And, to the same extent, we are able to reserve scientific extrapolations for our special study of what is not, or what is less than, fully human. The fact that we study those varieties of pathology that interfere with the achievement of human ends and so prevent men from becoming, in the full sense, human would seem to be a valid reason—indeed, the only valid reason—for studying man in the nonhuman terms of science, for compar-

[5] C. C. Jung, "Principles of Practical Psychotherapy," *Collected Works* (New York: Pantheon Books, 1954), 16, 3.

ing him to subhuman animals, to locomotives, or to electronic brains.

So, although it is chiefly on more public or official occasions that we pay our respects to the castle, the virtues of inconsistency are not without their dangers. There is first the danger that, growing weary of the split between our private and our public selves, we might try to heal it by surrendering our selves entirely to the system. But another danger, equally tempting, is that we might surrender both the system and our hard-won theories of psychopathology to one of those private, oversimplified dogmas of love that make up in fervor what they lack in content.

Like Pascal, I believe that it is perilous to remind man of his resemblance to the animals without at the same time reminding him of his greatness. If the psychiatrist cannot look to his own theory to find man's superiority to "other" natural objects and if common sense is too unreliable a guide, where can he turn? Certainly the practice of psychiatry requires some steady conception of the fully human. With this question, I turn now to the theories of Martin Buber—theories which, I think, provide an answer to the question, What is man? and at the same time add a new dimension to the concrete problems of psychiatry. This dimension may be called the *I–Thou.*

According to Buber, man's attitudes are twofold, in accordance with the twofold nature of the two primary words that he speaks in relation to the world. These are not isolate words, but combined words. One primary word is the combination *I–Thou.* The other primary word is the combination *I–It; He* or *She* may replace *It* without constituting, in Buber's terms, a change in this primary word. The *I* of man is also twofold, the *I* of *I–Thou* differing from the *I* of *I–It.* "Primary words do not signify things, but they intimate relations. . . . There is no *I* taken in itself, but only the *I* of the primary word *I–Thou* and *I* of the primary word *I–It*."[6]

The primary word *I–Thou* can only be spoken with the whole being, whereas the primary word *I–It* can never be spoken with the whole being. *I–Thou* is the primary word of relation, whereas *I–It* is the primary word of experiencing and using.

How can the *I–Thou* relation be described? Though it cannot, by definition, be an object of knowledge, there are qualities to the relation that can be recalled after the moment has subsided into the world of *It*. Since *I–Thou* can be spoken only with the whole being, it follows that the *I–Thou* relation is open, direct, and forthright—unobscured by such partial aspects of self-consciousness as shyness, envy, self-assertion, and the like. The *I–Thou* relation is mutual.

The *Thou* meets me. But I step into direct relation with him. Hence the relation means being chosen and choosing. . . . My *Thou* affects me, as I affect him.[7]

This should not be confused with the modern virtue called spontaneity. For a spontaneity that does not reckon with the *Thou* in his singularity, even as my *Thou* meets me, is mere self-indulgence, belonging to a far corner of the world of *It*. Nor should this mutual encounter be confused with empathy, which involves transporting oneself imaginatively into another being, event, or object, forfeiting one's own actuality. Nevertheless, such terms as empathy or rapport are often loosely used in an awkward effort to objectify the *I–Thou* relation.

The *I* of *I–It* has no present, only the past—and, by projection or prediction, the future. But "the *present* arises in

[6] Martin Buber, *I and Thou* (Edinburgh: T. & T. Clark, 1937), pp. 3–4.
[7] *Ibid.*, pp. 11–12.

virtue of the fact that the *Thou* becomes present." Of all the qualities of the *I–Thou* relation, presentness—the suspension of chronological time, the falling away of time past and time future—is the quality we all seek to invoke, in the absence of mutuality and directness, as a symbol of the *I–Thou* or as a first step toward relation. With boredom as the other side of presentness, all manner of distraction will suggest itself for "killing time," as we say—whereby, to quote Eliot, we are distracted from distraction by distraction. In lieu of relation, much of life can be exploited for the experience of presentness: laughter, tears, physical pain, anger, outrage, sleep, and sex. And perhaps the chemist's contributions ought to be included, too—alcohol, benzedrine, marijuana, and morphine —and, to stretch a point, the offerings of neurosurgery, lobotomy, and shock. The pursuit of presentness as an end in itself, without necessarily relinquishing hope of the *Thou*, would be described in current psychiatric theory under the heading of anxiety and defenses against anxiety—a formulation which, when hypostatized, can mistake the measure for the goal or the means for the end.

In addition to its directness, mutuality, and presentness, the *I–Thou* moment is *self-limited:* it cannot be sustained. "The exalted melancholy of our fate," according to Buber, lies in the fact that every *Thou* inevitably becomes an *It*. If we inspect the moment, it becomes an article of knowledge. If we attempt to extend the moment in whatever way—romantic or mystical—we are involved in the self-consciousness belonging to the world of *It*. Even to do nothing requires a self-conscious act of will.

The *Thou* of *I–Thou* is not restricted to men. The *I–Thou* relation may occur with nature, as well as with human artifacts and art forms. For here, too, there may be meeting and presentness, even though the meeting is neither with God nor with man. This is the feature of Buber's theory that extends the possibilities of *Thou* to all corners of exist-ence, so that the *Thou* may arise from almost any given aspect of life, public or private—provided one enters into the relation with his whole being. And since Buber, as might be anticipated, has been charged with pantheism or mysticism, I may quote his own words here. "Pantheism," he declared, "de-stroys or stunts the greatest of all values: the reciprocal rela-tionship between the human and the divine."[8] For him, in every *Thou*, in whatever sphere, "we look out toward the fringe of the eternal *Thou*, in each *Thou*, we address the eternal *Thou*."[9]

As I have already mentioned, *I–It* is the primary word of experiencing and using. Whether it occurs in terms of knowl-edge, feeling, or action, the *I–It* is the typical subject–other relationship of traditional epistemology, as well as of modern psychology. That is, the subject who knows is distinguished from the object that is known. Being thus mediate and in-direct, the *I–It* relationship also becomes "comprehensible and orderable." The *It* of *I–It* may equally well be a he, a she, an animal, a thing—even God—without a change in the primary word. Experience is *I–It*, whether it is the experi-encing of an object or of a man, whether it is "inner" or "outer," "open" or "secret." One's life of interior feeling is in no way elevated above one's life with the external world. Thus, Buber's terminology cuts across the usual distinctions in two ways. First, attention is focused upon the *relation-between* and not upon the individual object in its causal con-nections. Second, by relegating feelings to the world of *It*, Buber not only avoids the usual romantic over-valuation of "feeling," but also cuts through the usual dichotomy between thought and feeling.

[8] Buber, as quoted by Maurice S. Friedman in a letter to the author in 1956.
[9] *Op. cit.*, p. 101.

In psychiatry especially, there is an illusory opposition between so-called fact and so-called feeling. The therapists of a psychiatric hospital—more by virtue of temperament than theory—are apt to split into two seemingly opposing sides as they argue the quality or skill most conducive to recovery in their patients: the Oracles of Feeling are arrayed against the High Priests of Fact. The Oracles of Feeling apply to themselves such evocative terms from the age of romanticism as "warmth," "love," "intuition," "inspiration," and "empathy," whereas they indict their adversaries as "cold," "unfeeling," "intellectual," and "compulsive." From the other side, the High Priests of Fact pride themselves on their "objectivity," "judiciousness," "sobriety," and "scientific approach," whereas they accuse their opponents of being "mushy," "sentimental," "mindless," and "unscientific." The controversy between these two factions is like the familiar marital dilemma of soap opera: the conflict between the impractical wife who trusts what she feels, and her insensitive husband who knows a fact when he sees one.

For Buber, this war between sense and sensibility belongs to the world of *I–It*—a particular circumstance in which the *I* is held off from the *It,* the former inside and the latter outside, dividing the world conveniently into feelings and facts. If the argument is transposed figuratively from therapy and soap opera to the diagnostic categories of psychiatry, the dialogue now would be between the hysteric and the obsessional. For the hysteric, with his overblown sensibilities, a necessary step in treatment would be the acquisition of some logical capacity to deal with facts. And for the obsessional, the compulsion to free-associate might in itself furnish the beginnings of sensibility. Of these two extremes, Buber wrote:

But the separated *It* . . . is an animated clod without a soul, and the separated *I* of feelings an uneasily fluttering . . . bird. . . .

Neither of them knows man . . . or mutual life. . . . That feelings yield no personal life is understood only by a few. . . . If, like the modern man, you have learned to concern yourself wholly with your own feelings, despair at their unreality will not easily instruct you in a better way—for despair is also an interesting feeling.[10]

Thus Buber avoids the romantic attitude toward feeling that is peculiar to current philosophy. The romantic regards feeling as a spontaneous impulse arising either from above or from below: either as divine or poetic inspiration, or else as some daemonic force or instinct—as represented, for example, by the id. Buber rejected this kind of mysticism, with its Manichaean division between the forces of Light and Dark.

Buber's emphasis upon the relation between selves, rather than upon the individual self in its relations to the world, constitutes an obvious difference from Freudian psychology. His difference from Sullivanian psychology will become evident as a difference in the meaning assigned to the word relation. For example, when Buber spoke of the *I–Thou* as it may occur either in the young infant or among primitive races, it is clear that he was relying upon his own imagination to give him knowledge of these unknowable states of subjectivity. He was thus able to avoid the genetic fallacy that is common to all nineteenth-century psychology. This fallacy springs, like behaviorism, from a natural-science view of objects that is then applied to such invisible phenomena as human subjectivity or human experience. For example, when the nineteenth-century psychologist "looked at" an imaginary child or primitive, he was not imagining their experience, but quite literally visualizing an object: a bodily object, in its bodily behavior. Seen through the spectacles of natural-science theory, this bodily object would appear as a "natural object": a "human animal" or "organism." And, since he supposed the

[10] *Op. cit.*, p. 44.

origins of man's experience to lie in his bodily behavior, the psychologist could then suppose that the behavior of children, of primitives, and even of animals, would give him the "real" origins—and thence the "real truth"—about the whole of human experience. But the most striking fact about human experience is, of course, that so much of it is invisible.

As an example of the twin fallacies arising from this natural-science view of objects, Freud's view of the young child or primitive can be adduced. When he looked at the child's behavior, Freud saw megalomania, narcissism—libidinal drives operating in isolation, abstracted from the human experience. With this behaviorist view of motives, he sees "parental love," too, as something that is "touching" but is "at bottom . . . childish." Indeed Freud defines "parental love" as *"nothing but* parental narcissism born again."[11]

Here is an example of the genetic fallacy, according to which the supposed origins of parental love are somehow more real or important than the known experience of love, so that love becomes *nothing but* the narcissism of the child. This springs from the behaviorist fallacy, which claims that what cannot be seen or observed in a man's behavior cannot be known to man. As a further example of these two fallacies— which are, of course, equally reductive—I would like to quote Sullivan's definition of "tenderness" between a mother and her child: "My theorem is this: *The observed activity of the infant arising from the tension of needs induces tension in the mothering one, which tension is experienced as tenderness and as an impulsion to activities toward the relief of the infant's needs."*[12] This is a way of defining love as *nothing but* anxiety.

[11] Sigmund Freud, "On Narcissism: An Introduction," *Collected Papers* (New York: Basic Books, 1959) IV, 49. Italics mine.

[12] Harry Stack Sullivan, *The Interpersonal Theory of Psychiatry*, edited by Helen Swick Perry and Mary Ladd Gawel (New York: Norton, 1953), p. 39.

And an anxiety that needs to be relieved is not very different from an instinctual or libidinal drive that needs to be discharged. Thus, through these reductive views of man, current philosophy has arrived at both a biological and a steam-engine psychology of motives. Love is nothing but a physiological drive that needs outlet—nothing but an emotional tension that needs relief.

When Buber described those early or primitive experiences of the *Thou*, he was not looking at the behavior of the infant or its mother. Nor was he imagining any abstract relation that may exist between the two. He was rather imagining the experience of the mother toward her child, and of the child toward his mother. And he was imagining this to be a mutual experience of reciprocity—of shared relation. Buber therefore believed that human experience begins, both in the race and in the child, with relation. And, as I have already suggested, what he means by relation may be quite the opposite of what a psychiatrist means by the same word. For a relation imagined from the inside, as a mutual experience, is not the same thing as an abstract concept of relationship. The latter is "seen" or imagined from the outside, as an event occurring between two human objects.

Buber described the speech of primitive peoples as built up through acts that are charged with presentness. The Fuegian language, for example, has for the term *far away* a seven-syllable word meaning, "They stare at one another, each waiting for the other to volunteer to do what both wish and are not able to do."[13] But the *I–Thou* of the primitive man occurs before the separation and recognition of the *I*. With the separation of the human body as bearer of perceptions, with the world now as an object of perception, the primary word *I–It* comes into being, and with it causality. As with the primitive, so with the child: "In the beginning is relation . . .

[13] *Op. cit.*, p. 18.

the a priori of relation, *the inborn Thou.*" Like the primitive, the very young child, knowing no *I*, grasps the objects near him, with "the instinct to make everything into *Thou.*" Even his later games, in his "instinct to set up things in a synthetic or, if that is impossible, an analytic way, through pulling to pieces or tearing up, are also determined by the inborn *Thou*. His games express the longing for the *Thou.*" But, as the child becomes conscious of *I*, through the delimiting of his own body as perceiver and the subsequent comparison of his perceptions with the perceptions of others, he now utters *I–It*. That is, "he stands before things, but not over against them in the flow of mutual action." With this, the feeling of exclusiveness and universality disappears:

For the first time he experiences things as sums of qualities. . . . For the first time he sets things in time and space, in causal connection, each with its own place and appointed course, its measurability and conditioned nature. . . . The history of the individual and the human race indicates a progressive augmentation of the world of "it."[14]

The dimming of the inborn *Thou*, following the separation of the *I*, and the emergence of the world of *I–It*, is not intended as a psychological description of the development of the child or the race. But more detailed theories of psychopathology, whether they emphasize disturbances in libidinal development or the anxious relationship between parent and child, suggest the special morbid pathology that may disturb the ordinary course of development, as described by Buber, and that may cripple the child for later *I–Thou* relation. Whether the defect would consist of premature dispersion of the early *Thou* or later retardation of *I–It* experience, or both, cannot be said without microscopic examination of the particulars, insofar as this is possible.

[14] *Op. cit.*, pp. 28–30.

By now, it must be clear that Buber's theory of the two primary words bears some resemblance to Sullivan's interpersonal theory. Both appear to be social in nature—at least insofar as they regard the self as a series of dialogues. Both place a primary importance on the concept of relation, in some sense. But here the resemblance ends—not between the two men in their approach toward people, but between their two theories, as revealed by their very different terminologies. The view expressed—or, I would rather say, enforced—by Sullivan's language is often a physical-science view of objects, which is certainly not representative of his actual experience with people. No such split occurs, however, in Buber's language, which is always appropriate to man in his relations with the world. Sullivan's domain, of course, was psychopathology, or what is *not*-man, while Buber's domain is precisely what *is* man. To use Buber's own term for this, the study of "what is man?" may be called "philosophical anthropology." Finally, Sullivan made no claim to be religious, whereas Buber was a profoundly religious man.

Yet, even here the differences may be less great than the terminology would suggest. As Buber put it, the atheist who destroys idols in order that the spirit may be revived is acting in a more religious manner than the pious man who merely upholds the letter of religion. Sullivan worked devotedly to revive the smallest flickers of relationship, the faintest murmurs of the human, in that extreme situation known as schizophrenia. Buber's concept of relation between man and man came, of course, from the community life of Hasidic Jewry. But Sullivan, in his own way, strove equally to dispel that rabbinical aloofness—that distance placed between the omniscient "observer" and the lowly "subject"—which had afflicted psychiatrists in both their theory and their practice, reminding them that since involvement is inescapable, they had best admit it for scrutiny. Both men, in fact, abhorred the kind of analytical detachment that places the letter of the law above its spirit.

To describe those distortions in dialogue that are occasioned by the past, Sullivan used the word *parataxic*. Insisting that the psychiatrist could be no mere observer, since he was inevitably and inextricably involved with his patient, Sullivan coined the expression *participant observation* to describe the shift between involvement and scrutiny of the manner of involvement. Here he was hoping to break through, in his own way, the usual subject-object formulations of the past. At this point, however, unlike Buber, he saw his larger framework in the operational field theories of the physical sciences. Early in his career, he adopted another term, *consensual validation*, to indicate agreement on the terms of dialogue by the participants. Underlying his theory, then, is a norm or goal having to do with the capacity for communication, whether verbal or nonverbal. Thus, it is no accident that many communications engineers or cyberneticists should, like many social scientists, find support in Sullivan's theories.

But of this type of social communication or sociality, Maurice S. Friedman writes:

It is important . . . not to lose sight of the fact that though the world of the *It* is a social world which is derived from the world of the *Thou*, it often sets itself up as the *final reality*. Its sociality, as a result, becomes largely "technical dialogue" . . . the mere communication and interaction between human beings who may in fact largely relate to each other as *It*'s.[15]

For Buber, the goal of all dialogue is the *Thou* relation, toward which "consensually validated" communication must of course assist. The difference between the two men lies as much in their approach to language as in their approach to subjectivity. For while Sullivan felt that subjective relations could be studied from the objective viewpoints of a scientist

[15] Maurice S. Friedman, "Buber's Theory of Knowledge," *Rev. of Metaphysics*, 8 (1954), 264–280.

—moreover, of a physical scientist—and that experience could be adequately described in the terminology of the sciences, Buber knew that language may not only determine our concepts but radically change our experiences as well.

It has been said that psychoanalytic candidates temporarily forfeit their therapeutic powers during their training period, when they try to bend their ordinary language to the technical principles taught them. Although training must have some such hybridizing effect on the students of all professions, I believe that the young psychoanalyst suffers most cruelly as —for the second time in his life—he learns to talk. Although definitions of psychoanalysis as treatment differ considerably, they do agree on the radical importance of interpretation. And whether the interpretation consists of silence, sighing, grunting, questioning, repetition, or revelation, language will be crucially involved. For that matter, it is easy to forget that even listening requires something more than remaining mute while looking attentive—namely, it requires the ability to attend imaginatively to another's language. Whenever the paraphernalia of psychoanalysis—the couch, the silence, the impassivity—are affected merely as a matter of style, they then become the acting-out of a charade around the word listening. Actually, in listening we speak the other's words. Or, to put it in another way, the analyst is able to hear only what he, potentially at least, is able to say.

Interpretation, then, would express the analyst's own reworking in language of that attention to the other's existence out of which relation might arise. The impairment of language, both in listening and talking, would prevent relation and be inimical to therapy. Of course, the candidate need not be permanently crippled by his education. Recovery will come when he has translated the instruction of his professors into his own language, shedding en route all those evasions of thinking that make up technical jargon. In a way, analytic interpretation resembles, for better or for worse, various older

145

forms of interpretation. As in the exegesis of historical or religious documents, the analyst is revising old or dead forms of the letter in the light of contemporary existence. Thus, the ideal interpretation would perhaps be one in which the commentary was so perspicaciously ordered as to provide both a relevant message and a suitable form of address as well. It would combine both knowing-about and knowing—both *It* and *Thou*. Certainly it is only when a *Thou* relation arises out of interpretation that the patient will risk the pain of applying this interpretation to further explorations of his disorder. For although he may be willing to undergo all the usual social deprivation that distinguishes the analytic relationship from mere friendship, he would be less or more than human if he could exist without hope of the *Thou*.

It is easy to see how many busy, useful lives are given over to a mastery or enjoyment of the world of the *It* at the expense of the *Thou*. Buber wrote, "And in all the seriousness of truth, hear this: without *It* man cannot live. But he who lives with *It* alone is not a man."[16] But it is just as easy to find bohemians and romantics—misguided poets or religionists of all kinds—who make the opposite mistake, pursuing the *Thou* at the expense of the *It*. Buber himself was suspicious of all prescriptions for the *Thou* relation—especially those of certain brands of mysticism, scientism, and romanticism—which, while charting their ecstatic course, evade the concrete details of existence. The result of such prescriptions is blasphemous: a pseudo-*Thou*, an *It* addressed as *Thou*, betraying the realities of both worlds.

Such a formulation might describe those dubious therapeutic experiences, usually hysterical, in which the patient addresses his physician as *Thou*, without prior relation having occurred. In such a pact, the manner of address may be required by the form of the therapy itself, as in hypnosis. Or, it may

[16] *Op. cit.*, p. 34.

be more subtly incited, in the equalitarian therapies, by the needs of one or both parties to the experience. In any case, however it comes about that the physician is addressed as *Thou*, the fact that he must continue to be addressed as *Thou* soon constitutes a more deadly disability for the patient than any symptom that may have disappeared in the process. In this state of pseudograce, no fact may be admitted which challenges the *It* addressed as *Thou*, and with such atrophy in the world of *It*, the possibility of a *Thou* relation diminishes. In the hysterical enterprise, it is sex and sexual metaphor that so willfully force the pseudo-*Thou*. Thus, what was formerly one of the expressions of relation or love becomes an idolatry, fragmented endlessly in the world of *It*—each article of the sexual act carrying the willful burden. In a sexological age where man is defined by his sexual competence, love has been relegated to a device for achieving orgasm. Here Buber may be quoted on the "erotic man":

Many years I have wandered through the land of men, and have not yet reached an end of studying the varieties of the "erotic man." . . . There a lover stamps around and is in love only with his passion. There one is wearing his differentiated feelings like medal ribbons. There one is enjoying the adventures of his own fascinating effect. There one is gazing enraptured at the spectacle of his own supposed surrender. There one is collecting excitement. There one is displaying his "power." There one is preening himself with borrowed vitality. There one is delighting to exist simultaneously as himself and as an idol very unlike himself. There one is warming himself at the blaze of what has fallen to his lot. There one is experimenting. And so on and on—all the manifold monologists with their mirrors, in the apartment of the most intimate dialogue. . . .[17]

Buber's thought can help us as psychiatrists, I believe, not only in providing a general framework against which to measure the special virtues and limitations of our special craft,

[17] Martin Buber, *Between Man and Man* (New York: Macmillan, 1948), p. 29.

but also in revising some of the most technical or specific details of our craft. The mistake is often made, especially with the schizophrenic, of overvaluing his lonely gropings toward the *Thou* and of underestimating his actual incompetence in the world of *It*, so that he becomes a tragic saint or poet of the *Thou*, martyred by the world of *It*.

Once it is realized, however, that the *Thou* relation depends upon the world of *It* for its conceptual forms or meanings, then psychosis can be seen as not only a failure of the *Thou*—of so-called personal relations. It is an equal failure of knowledge, judgment, and experience in the world of *It*. Whatever class the disorder falls into—whether it is marked by a recoil from relations, as in schizophrenia, or by a grasping at relation, as in hysteria or mania—underlying its manifestations one can always find much ignorance of the world, much ineptitude with people, much early failure to acquire the elementary tools of knowledge.

If schizophrenia can be thought of as an extreme withering of the *Thou* capacity, with corresponding impairment in the world of *It*, it is not surprising that it should be accompanied by a crippling of the intellect. I mean intellect not in the narrow sense of a measurable reason or intelligence, but in a larger sense—experience informed with imagination, and imagination ordered by knowledge and judgment.

In a Rorschach study of schizophrenia that is not yet published, Margaret Rioch has found the prospects for recovery poorest whenever the patient's intellectual and imaginative powers are most severely limited. And Donald L. Burnham has observed that we psychiatrists tend to underestimate the literal-mindedness of the schizophrenic, arising from this same defect of imagination, so that we attribute to him far greater powers of metaphor or symbolism than he possesses.[18] Al-

[18] Donald L. Burnham, "Some Problems in Communication with Schizophrenic Patients," *J. Amer. Psychoanal. Assn.*, 3 (1955), 67–81.

though much of the romanticism about the creativity of the schizophrenic stems from this overestimation of his imaginative powers, at least it is a benevolent mistake that often helps him to widen the areas of his experience and knowledge. For without sufficient knowledge, memory, or judgment, every *Thou* invoked is apt to be a perilously shy and fleeting one. It recedes very quickly into its impoverished world of *It*, where there is little promise of return. And with each loss of the *Thou*, the schizophrenic is in special danger of retreating more permanently or deeply toward his far pole of alienation: into that loneliness of which both Sullivan and Fromm-Reichmann have written.

Psychiatry owes both these therapists a debt for adding so untechnical a term as loneliness to our technical vocabulary. Such loneliness might, in Buber's language, be called hopeless longing for the *Thou*, and so might be seen as the despair that afflicts all of us at moments, and overwhelms the more desperate ones we call psychotic. Even that mad chattering by which we detain an unwelcome guest at his moment of departure—even that madder chattering by which the "manic" patient detains all humanity as his parting guest—is this not a desperate or guilty recognition that the whole social enterprise, the whole wedding of minds, has been a total failure? We strive wildly on the doorstep for one departing *Thou*.

What is called fear of intimacy in the schizophrenic might be more accurately called the fear of losing intimacy. And the wilder manias of pseudointimacy, which serve as a desperate camouflage for hopelessness, could also be seen as desperate gambits to retrieve what never has been gained. It cannot be denied that the strained smile or the joyless laughter, that often substitutes for friendship at a dinner party, bears some relation to the giggling of a hebephrenic or the grimace of catatonics. Such temporary despair as may overtake a guest when thrust into postures of intimacy with a stranger might

149

easily be the permanent despair of those who live in exile from the human state.

To speak only of the schizophrenic, he feels, of course, that having lost all hope or chance of intimacy, any further efforts will only carry him further out of paradise. He fears, in other words, that should his loneliness be entered momentarily by a "thou," the ensuing loss—the return, empty-handed, to his vacant world of "it"—would be more than he could endure. Since he can neither take it with him, nor find it there on his arrival, the schizophrenic exiles himself from both earth and heaven and, with a surprising dignity, takes up his residence in limbo.

In view of his circumstances, therefore, we psychiatrists can admire his most bizarre visions or venturings as instances of some enterprise and courage. Indeed, we owe this admiration to such therapists as Sullivan and Fromm-Reichmann. So when the man who has just saved the White House from invasion is sent to us for correction, we are not likely to forget the nobility of his motives and intentions. But we may be in some danger of forgetting the sheer absurdity, in worldly terms, of both his thinking and his actions. We may forget that all the melodramas called psychotic stem from a double failure in the double world of man's existence.

And here is the crux of the therapeutic problem, which is also the crux of the human problem. It is the duality of being human that accounts for the two kinds of knowledge, the two kinds of reality, the two kinds of thought and speech. The mode of speech appropriate to being human is not the mode appropriate to human objects. Having used only the single mode of scientific knowledge for the past hundred years or so, we are uneasily aware that this was the wrong mode—the wrong viewpoint, the wrong terminology, and the wrong kind of knowledge—ever to explain the human being. The results of this wrongness are only now becoming obvious, as we find everything human being treated as an object of study and control, whether by medical, political, or social engineers. Man himself has become that single object, that single organism that is studied differently by every science. And however the organism is described—whether as an animal to be improved, or as a body to be kept healthy by such remedies as love; whether as a brain to be cured by convulsions or by surgery, or as an organic cell within a giant State, controlled by twentieth-century methods both political and scientific—it remains a construct which has little to do with being human.

But if we think of psychiatry as something designed for human beings, and not for human organisms, then we can see that the human condition has not been radically altered by the social or even the psychiatric improvements of the past few centuries. Nor have the human states of error, misery, or despair been altered much by calling them neurotic or psychotic states of illness. Although the new vocabulary has brought some radical changes or improvements in their cure, their causes have not altered radically. The therapeutic problem remains the human problem. And although few would claim that problems of moral or mental or spiritual sickness can be abstracted from values of morality or intellect or spirit as a whole, we must consider whether a violent separation or abstraction from the whole has not, in fact, been accomplished through language—through the increasing application of a medical or scientific terminology to describe the whole of man's existence.

To say that the therapist can invoke, under certain conditions, a fleeting relation with the most dilapidated hebephrenic is only to say that anyone can invoke, under similar conditions, a fleeting relation with anyone, from the most hardened criminal to the most frivolous of sinners. How far this relation, once invoked, can be established on some reliable basis will depend largely upon those qualities of judgment, knowledge, and critical discrimination that are generally called intellectual qualities—although they might equally well be called those of common sense. I suppose we can agree that common sense—common sense at its best, at any rate—is composed of those Western, Christian values which are largely Greek and Jewish in their origins. While common sense is generally mixed, in any age, with much recent nonsense, it does tend on the whole to preserve only the best of what is ancient. And what it preserves is not only the general principles of morality and religion, but also a large body of concrete knowledge concerning the life of man.

It is this kind of knowledge, of the specifically human kind, which I have tried to distinguish here from the scientific knowledge of man. For the latter is, of course, mixed with a great deal of scientific knowledge about the nonhuman worlds of nature and the universe. Needless to say, a knowledge of the nonhuman is apt to become a dangerous pseudo-knowledge when applied to man.

Whereas psychoanalytic practice may be a blend of medicine and common sense, the practice of neurology and neurosurgery may rest on nothing more than scientific knowledge —split off completely from common-sense or humanist traditions. Psychoanalysis has, of course, done a great deal to heal this split. Most of us can remember a time when mental illness, or diseases of the nervous system, were thought to be a special invention of the nineteenth century—farther removed in spirit from the general condition of humanity than any lunatic chained in Bedlam. For the eighteenth-century lunatic was, after all, removed only bodily from society; he was not exiled spiritually from the human race. Through such efforts as those of Fromm-Reichmann and Sullivan, the schizophrenic has now been restored to the human state.

While Freud in his practice had earlier done much to heal the split, it must be admitted that his theories have done much to widen it. If the nervous patient was restored to humanity as a neurotic—only slightly more deranged than the rest of mankind and somewhat less deranged than society itself—this was not accomplished without a certain cost. We could now regard our moral, intellectual, and spiritual failures with a greater sympathy or indulgence, not to say complacency, but the price paid for this was to define ourselves altogether in medical terms of health or illness—according to the relative presence or absence of neurosis. So, if all our sins or crimes could now be excused on medical or social grounds, most of our greatest triumphs and achievements could also be explained, and even excused, on the same grounds of illness. The new criteria of emotional maturity or social health were not favorable to fanatics, rebels, prophets, or revolutionists —unless, of course, they happened to be political revolutionists of a certain humanitarian color.

It is for this reason—because everything uniquely human has been translated into medical terms of illness—that the psychoanalyst is now carrying such a heavy burden of responsibility. He no longer deals merely with problems of medical ethics, or with the moral problems arising from his craft. Morality itself has been turned over to him, along with philosophy and religion. It is not only his patients who ask him to solve their moral and religious problems, to tell them what is human. Nor is it only the artist, the philosopher, the teacher who turns to him; moralists and priests and theologians are now turning to the psychoanalyst for their definitions of man. Needless to say, we never asked for a burden of power such as this, which amounts to our taking over the sole responsibility for the human fate. Yet it is the scientist, and not the layman, who must be blamed for this astonishing situation. For it is the medical man's delusion that psychiatry deals not with moral errors, sins, and weakness—not with intellectual failures and with spiritual states of grace or vanity or despair—but only with a special pocket of ailments whose cure and cause lie far outside the realm of moral values. So, if the theologian applies to the psychiatrist for his diagnosis of despair or sin, it is because he has no idea that he is doing so. He believes he is asking merely for a medical opinion on disease.

My hope, in presenting the thoughts of a Jewish philosopher —who was also a moralist, a theologian, a poet, a psychologist, an historian, a critic, and above all, a religious man—is partly the hope that we psychoanalysts may turn over some of our unwanted burden to those who are better qualified, by their education, than we are. To select a Jewish theologian is not to imply that similar thoughts cannot be found among the Christians, especially among those who subscribe to that religious humanism that is now called existentialist. For me, however, Buber has provided a peculiar relevance which I have not found elsewhere. He was familiar enough with psychiatry to be able to distinguish between its theory and its practice, and thus to distinguish the moral contributions offered, especially by psychoanalytic practice, from the follies and dangers inherent in our theories and our scientific terminology. Thus, although he was well aware, as a theologian, that psychiatry deals with the same realms of spirit as his own, as a poet he was equally, and most unusually, aware of the difference which language makes. The man who describes a human meeting in the language appropriate to such meetings is simply not talking about the same thing as the man who describes the interrelatedness of organisms. So in this sense, and only in this sense, it is true to say that psychiatry deals with special ailments of the organism which have nothing to do with human beings. Fortunately, what this means is that it is not the scientist himself, but only the language of science that is far removed from human history.

8

THE THERAPEUTIC
DESPAIR

The wounded surgeon plies the steel
That questions the distempered part;
Beneath the bleeding hands we feel
The sharp compassion of the healer's art
Resolving the enigma of the fever chart.

Our only health is the disease
If we obey the dying nurse
Whose constant care is not to please
But to remind of our, and Adam's curse,
And that, to be restored, our sickness must
grow worse.

The whole earth is our hospital
Endowed by the ruined millionaire,
Wherein, if we do well, we shall
Die of the absolute paternal care
That will not leave us, but prevents us ev-
erywhere.

—T. S. ELIOT[1]

I wish to speak here of the anomalous situation by which the field of psychotherapy exists as a kind of crossbreed between medical science and something very different from science; and of the necessary and needless hardships which this anomaly imposes on the therapist, especially in working with schizophrenia. In using the word *despair*, I mean to suggest first that, given the situation of the therapist, some despair is inevitable; second, that despair itself may have a therapeutic value which has been overlooked.

The anomalous situation was created, of course, with Freud.

[1] T. S. Eliot, "East Coker," *Four Quartets* (New York: Harcourt, Brace, 1943), pp. 15-16.

His introduction of a close, prolonged, and intense relationship with a patient for several hours a week—and extending often over a period of years—meant a novelty so unprecedented in the medical sciences as virtually to remove psychotherapy from the field of science altogether. Since the kind of interpersonal relation which developed out of this is without parallel in medicine, even in the closest friendship with a family physician, psychiatrists have had to look for parallels outside the sciences: in the general field of education, including moral and religious instruction. More recently some of us were made aware through Martin Buber's visit in Washington in 1957, that a field of inquiry with great relevance to our own exists under the term "philosophical anthropology," devoting itself to the question, What is man?

Here I would like to borrow from Buber one concept having to do with his theory of "confirmation." By confirmation, he means simply

. . . the wish of every man to be confirmed as what he is, even as what he can become, by men; and the innate capacity in man to confirm his fellow-men in this way.[2]

The complete realization of such mutual confirmation is a rare event, yet its *partial* fulfillment is frequent enough in ordinary life. The capacity for confirming and being confirmed depends, according to Buber, on what he calls "imagining the real."

Applied to intercourse between men, "imagining" the real means that I imagine to myself what another man is at this very moment wishing, feeling, perceiving, thinking, and not as a detached content but in his very reality, that is, as a living process in this man.[3]

The need to be confirmed as what one is, "even as what he can become"—this need would seem indisputable in one's

[2] Martin Buber, "Distance and Relation," *Psychiatry*, 20 (1957), 97–104; p. 102.
[3] *Ibid.*, p. 103.

ordinary existence. But in the extraordinary existence that is psychotherapy, the therapist is concerned only with the patient's need for confirmation, often at the expense of his own. A need too drastically thwarted may become a sort of craving that, if unrecognized, will lead either to despair or to illusion: provoking, instead of confirmation, its own mirage.

Here I should like to distinguish a genuine despair, which is an appropriate response to this lack of confirmation, from another and more useless kind that may be only an avoidance of that response. It may arise solely from false goals or from mistaken optimism concerning the nature and ends of therapy. In particular, there is a dangerous optimism that is created all too easily from the central illusion of our calling. This illusion is twofold: it asserts, first, that psychology is or ought to be an exact science, and, second, that exact sciences are those that do not require imagination.

It is not merely to find the origins of this illusion, but to understand its nature, that one must go back to Freud's own conception of psychotherapy as a science modeled, both in theory and in practice, on the natural and physical sciences.

Freud himself may be held responsible for one of the chief immodesties of this psychoanalytic age: namely, for the presumption that one can, instead of imagining, actually know the other in his essence. Although he himself was one of the great imaginative geniuses of the age, Freud warred consistently against imagination, which he equated with "illusion." As Will Herberg has written, "Reason is Freud's god, and truth—which he identifies with scientific truth—the only epiphany he recognizes."[4] There is little point, at this stage, in belaboring the crudities of Freud's conception of "religion" —rather, of pseudo-religion—which he shared, after all, with the scientific rationalism of his day. But "religion" was not the only great illusion from which he found mankind suffering.

[4] Will Herberg, "Freud, Religion, and Social Reality," *Commentary*, 23 (March 1957), No. 3, pp. 277–284.

Art and philosophy provided two other comforting "illusions" that also compensated man for the instinctual sacrifices exacted of him by a repressive civilization.

Now such a view of natural instinct at war with human civilization is, of course, pure romanticism. For like most of the great naturalists of the nineteenth century, Freud combined a romantic and almost mystical celebration of instinct with an equal reverence for its logical opposite: that is, for reason, defined as scientific truth. And here the definition was as candidly naturalistic as a camera: truth was the "correspondence [of scientific thought] with the real external world."[5]

While this may be called "rationalism," it nevertheless represents an irrational elevation—almost a divinization—of the outer world as the only reliable source of knowledge. Fortunately, however, such a thoroughgoing exaltation of the outer or visible world at the expense of inner truth is almost impossible to put into practice. In practice, subjectivity, common sense—imagination itself—were all smuggled into the Freudian therapy under some rather conflicting terms of natural science. And although this had the welcome result of bestowing on subjectivity a little of that intellectual prestige previously enjoyed only by scientific "objectivity," other results were less fortunate. In particular, I should class it as a misfortune that so many intellectual processes and values, so many esthetic or philosophical or religious meanings, had now to be translated into vague romantic terms of natural "feeling," or else into the less vague but equally romantic terms of natural "instinct."

As an example of this intellectual impoverishment, which was at the same time a narrowing of experience, I should like to return to Freud's evaluation of art and philosophy. If these were illusory or unreal compared to "real" scientific knowl-

[5] Sigmund Freud, "A Philosophy of Life," in *New Introductory Lectures on Psychoanalysis* (New York: Norton, 1933), p. 233.

edge, it must be remembered that this kind of positivism was by no means unique to Freud, but characterized the dominant philosophy of his day. As for art, he considered it "harmless" and even "beneficent," since

... it does not seek to be anything else but an illusion. Save in the case of a few people ... obsessed by Art, it never dares to make any attacks on the realm of reality.[6]

Here he was not, of course, speaking of those comfortable pseudo-arts which are popular precisely because they do not attack any conventional notions of "reality." He was speaking of *Lear* and *Hamlet*. Of *Hamlet* he said (writing, for some reason, anonymously):

I have followed the literature of psychoanalysis closely, and I accept its claim that it was not until the material of the tragedy had been traced back analytically to the Oedipus theme that the mystery of its effect was at last explained.[7]

Here, in such reductive "explanations" of a work of art, is a good example of that genetic fallacy which always explains the nature of a hen by calling her an egg. Even when it came to more humble forms of literary art, such as wit or humor, Freud's genetic explanations had necessarily to reduce all intellectual or aesthetic values to the level of a nonverbal wish or preintellectual condition. As may be observed in the portions I have italicized below, the following explanation of "humor" seems actually to define it as the opposite of humor:

Now that we have *reduced the mechanism of* humoristic pleasure *to a formula of comic pleasure* and of wit, *we are at the end of our task.* ... The pleasure of wit originates from an *economy of expenditure* in inhibition, of the comic from an *economy of expenditure* in *thought,* and of humor from an *economy of expenditure* in *feeling.* All three modes ... strive to bring back ... a

[6] *Ibid.*, p. 219.
[7] Sigmund Freud, "The Moses of Michelangelo," *Collected Papers* (New York: Basic Books, 1959), IV, 259.

pleasure . . . lost . . . a bygone time . . . the state of our childhood in which we *did not know the comic*, were *incapable of wit*, and *did not need humor* to make us happy.[8]

Here one can see the nature of the genetic fallacy, which does not claim that art is nothing but a childish motive; nor does it claim that man is nothing but an animal or a child. What it does is more insidious. It first explains an intellectual pursuit entirely in nonintellectual terms of motive; and, secondly, explains the motive entirely in terms of animal "instinct" or of infantile "feeling." And it was from such unrecognized or subtle forms of reduction that Freud seems to have derived his definition of philosophy as a childish "illusion."

Still, if "philosophy . . . clings to the illusion that it can produce a complete and coherent picture of the universe,"[9] this was a relatively harmless illusion, like the illusions of art, when compared to the really dangerous myths of religion:

Of the three forces which can dispute the position of science, religion alone is a really serious enemy.[10]

Without going into Freud's criticism of philosophy, which is neither very perceptive nor very well-informed, one can see that his chief fire was reserved for any system of meanings which dared to set itself up in competition with Science. Science alone was able to produce a complete and coherent picture of the universe, from which to deduce—in more or less identical terms—a complete and coherent science of man. Now this may be called positivism, or it may be called the omniscient approach to man. In terms of omniscience, it has been well and sufficiently criticized by latterday psycho-

[8] Sigmund Freud, "Wit and the Various Forms of the Comic," *The Basic Writings of Sigmund Freud*, translated and edited by A. A. Brill (New York: Modern Library, 1938), p. 803.
[9] Sigmund Freud, "A Philosophy of Life," in *New Introductory Lectures on Psychoanalysis* (New York: Norton, 1933), pp. 219–220.
[10] *Ibid.*, p. 219.

analysts, as well as by modern physicists; indeed, it was to get away from the "omniscient observer" of old-fashioned science that Harry Stack Sullivan introduced the notion, derived from modern physics, of the "participant observer."[11]

Yet I think that this question of omniscience, or "playing God," does not get to the heart of the problem. It would be more relevant to ask, In what terms is the omniscience conceived or described? Is it the omniscience of a physical scientist or is it the omniscience, for instance, of an artist or of a benevolent god? *Any* complete or coherent system of meanings by which man finds it necessary to live will require him to see himself whole, in a manner which could be called omniscient or even godlike. The question for philosophical anthropology is not whether such imagined viewpoints are omniscient, but whether they are relevant: whether they are true in the sense of being appropriate to man's existence; true in the sense of being useful or benevolent, conducive to a "human" way of life. And this comes down to a question of language, for man can see himself, as well as speak of himself, in terms of the natural or physical science, or in some other terms. He *sees* himself by means of the language that defines him as a man and, of course, he behaves accordingly.

Thus, while psychotherapists have leaned over backwards —one could almost say have stood on their heads—in the effort to correct their scientific impulse toward omniscience, they have never, I think, discriminated between one kind of omniscience and another, nor between the kind of language appropriate to each. For this reason I believe that we, as psychotherapists, have not sufficiently questioned the appropriateness of using scientific terms to define our work, our patients, and ourselves. Certainly in Freud's case we do not

[11] Harry Stack Sullivan, *The Interpersonal Theory of Psychiatry*, edited by Helen Swick Perry and Mary Ladd Gawel (New York: Norton, 1953), pp. 13-14.

appreciate his real and unique value until we have performed a fairly thorough job of translation—or what amounts to the same thing—until we have disengaged his valuable insights into *human* nature from all those naturalist and romantic theories about nature itself in which they are embedded. Until we make this translation, from the natural into the human, Freud's enormous prestige among the very groups he attacked—the artists, the philosophers, and the religionists—remains mysterious indeed. As Lionel Trilling has put it: "Freud . . . has much to tell us about art, but whatever is suggestive in him is not likely to be found in those of his works in which he deals expressly with art itself."[12] Nevertheless,

It was left for Freud to discover how, in a scientific age, we still feel and think in figurative formations, and to create, what psychoanalysis is, a science of tropes, of metaphor and its variants. . . .[13]

In other words, when Freud is approached, not as a scientist investigating the nature of the organism, but rather as a critic investigating the nature of language and imagination, then, ironically enough, his great value as an imaginative, and even poetic, genius becomes apparent. Psychotherapists may wonder what relation "a science of tropes" or of metaphor bears to their own science. But, to turn for a moment to Freud's psychotherapy, it can easily be seen what effect his language—the terms he chose for defining his science—have had upon our own.

Above, I spoke of the immodest effort to "know," rather than to "imagine," what the patient in his essence is. Because scientists have imagined that no valid source of knowledge could be found in imagination, psychoanalysts, beginning with Freud, have made heroic efforts to deny the sources of much

[12] Lionel Trilling, *The Liberal Imagination* (New York: The Viking Press, 1950), p. 42.
[13] *Ibid.*, p. 53.

of their own knowledge, with the result that imagination has had to be smuggled into the halls of science through the janitor's entrance. And even there it could not be admitted for what it is, but has had to be heavily draped and veiled as something more respectable: namely, scientific reason.

Freud's insistent claim to be a man of science, offering only the most empirical facts about the human psyche, has misled nearly everyone, beginning with himself. And yet in 1900 he wrote with a surprising frankness: ". . . I am not really a man of science, not an observer, not an experimenter, and not a thinker. I am nothing but by temperament a *conquistador*—an adventurer . . . with the curiosity, the boldness, and the tenacity that belongs to that type of being."[14] In his case histories, it can be seen that it was just this tenacity and boldness which gave him the imaginative freedom to pursue his theories, often in the teeth of facts. He had none of that scholar's caution, that timidity of the scientist or historian or lawyer, that sticks to the rules of evidence, no matter what the cost. Freud, without knowing it, was a poet. He put no real trust in the fallible laws and man-made facts of evidence. What he was after was always the pure ideal, the pure imagined ideal: the truth itself. Here I do not mean to praise the poets above the scholars; usually the poets have as much power of mischief as of good— a power that many scholars will spend many years trying vainly to undo. Every poet is a grand conquistador, although not every poet dreams of scientific conquest. Listen to Freud's cry of anguished indignation when this dream is frustrated and Dora refuses, vengefully, to continue treatment:

Dora had listened to me without any of her usual contradictions. She seemed to be moved; she said good-bye to me very warmly, with the heartiest wishes for the New Year, and—came no more. . . . I knew Dora would not come back again. Her breaking off so

14 Ernest Jones, *The Life and Work of Sigmund Freud*, (New York: Basic Books, 1953), 1, 348.

The Ways of the Will

unexpectedly, just when my hopes of a successful termination of the treatment were at their highest, and her thus bringing those hopes to nothing—this was an unmistakable act of vengeance on her part.[15]

Out of this defeat, however, were to come his insights into those idolatrous aspects of romance which he called "transference." Concerning Dora, for example:

Might I perhaps have kept the girl under my treatment if I myself had acted a part, if I had exaggerated the importance to me of her staying on, and had shown a warm personal interest in her—a course which, even after allowing for my position as her physician, would have been tantamount to providing her with a substitute for the affection she longed for? I do not know.[16]

But "No one who, like me, conjures up the most evil of those half-tamed demons that inhabit the human breast, and seeks to wrestle with them, can expect to come through the struggle unscathed."[17]

If few of his papers begin without some heroic claim to total certainty or perfect knowledge, few of them end without some inspired abandonment of all scientific pretense. Whenever the facts were contradicted by a theory, Freud was always ready to abandon them—not often frankly, however. "The Psychogenesis of a Case of Homosexuality in a Woman," for example, begins like any work of art with the author's promise, at least implied, that he is about to tell the whole truth so far as he is able.[18] But as expressed in the positivist terms of science—rather of historical determinism—this promise takes on a rather comical sort of omniscience: that is to

[15] Sigmund Freud, "Analysis of a Case of Hysteria," *Collected Papers* (New York: Basic Books, 1959), III, 131.

[16] *Ibid.*, p. 132.

[17] *Ibid.*, pp. 131–132.

[18] Sigmund Freud, "The Psychogenesis of a Case of Homosexuality in a Woman," *Collected Papers* (New York: Basic Books, 1959), II, 202.

say, omniscience of an inappropriate or even impossible kind that might, in this instance, be called the historian's omniscience. For the author tells us that he has been able to trace the whole "origin, and development" of this case "with complete certainty and almost without a gap."[19] The comedy broadens as the many gaps in this case history become so apparent, even to the historian, that he now has to justify his "meager information." This he does on at least four grounds, three of which must surely be superfluous. The alibis range, with a refreshing absence of logic, from "medical discretion" and premature termination of analysis to the suggestion that all homosexuals are liars anyhow!

From a scientific viewpoint such illogic may seem disingenuous, especially since a whole theory of homosexuality has been built on the testimony of this patient who is so airily discredited as a liar. But from another viewpoint, it can be seen that Freud has done something far more interesting and important than to "trace the whole origin and development of a case." Instead, he has offered many profoundly useful insights into that human kind of history that has nothing to do with medical or natural history, and into the human kind of nature that has nothing to do with the "real external world" and may, perhaps, be entirely false to that nonhuman world. Insofar as these insights must be called true, I should like to call them facts: facts that are no less real or imagined than those which science has defined as facts, but which obey different laws and concern quite another subject than do the facts of nature.

In the case above, as so often happens, it was just at this moment of his greatest scientific defeat that Freud's imagination came brilliantly to the rescue, offering to his intellect many ingenious insights and a few profound truths by which

19 *Ibid.*, p. 202.

165

to explain his "failure." Unfortunately, the truths were unacceptable to his intellect or training until he had reshaped them into the clumsy "facts" of medical history. As though suspecting the role played by imagination in all mental processes, he explicitly denies it as follows:

The network of causes and effects that I shall now proceed to lay bare is not a product of my gift for combination; it is based on such trustworthy analytic evidence that I can claim objective validity for it. . . .[20]

And indeed an objective validity can be found for all of Freud's important insights, although not where he sought it— not in that "network of cause and effect" that he proudly imagined himself to be laying bare.

Returning now to my immediate concern, the point I wish to make here is simply the extent to which we psychotherapists may have retained—not omniscience—but some of the viewpoints more proper to a study of nature than of man.

We have abandoned most of the goals of positivist science, although we still cling to many of the positivist assumptions. Although we still hope to trace the whole origin and development of a case, as though plotting the course of a disease, we no longer hope to know everything with "complete certainty" and without a single gap. The sad lesson we have learned here might even be attributed to simple discouragement, rather than to any radical examination of our goal. We no longer hope to be omniscient, although omniscience is the unattainable goal of intellect or knowledge, just as perfect goodness is the absolute ideal of morality or religion. Christians were enjoined to imitate Christ, in the full knowledge that success was forever impossible. The blasphemy or despair issues not from the pursuit of impossible goals, but only from forgetting their impossibility: forgetting the difference be-

[20] *Ibid.*, p. 213.

tween an ideal and a fact. And this is what positivism, like many Christian heresies, forgot. Out of the heresy comes either the lunatic belief that one is God, perfectly good, perfectly omniscient or omnipotent, or else the lunatic despair that one is not.

The temptations of omniscience in the treatment of schizophrenia have been frequently remarked on in the psychoanalytic literature. It has been said, for example, that since it takes a thief to catch a thief, psychotherapists must begin with a bit of the disease they would treat. Or, that the disorder is so resistant to treatment and therefore so wounding to the therapist's ambitions, that it is difficult for him not to respond with grandiosity. Perhaps the most common theory—and one that smacks of black magic—is that it is dangerous to expose oneself to the unconscious of the schizophrenic, since the resultant anxiety might be severe enough to cause disorder in the therapist.

There may be a measure of truth to all the explanations cited, yet I believe that Buber's theory of confirmation can shed particular light upon these hazards by helping to distinguish between therapeutic dialogue and what he calls "genuine dialogue." As a quotidian affair stretching painfully through the years, the psychotherapy of schizophrenia has simply not been truthfully described. Reports not only give it an order and meaning that it does not possess; they also deprive it of the brutal tedium, exasperation, emptiness, futility —in short, the agony of existence in which dialogue is so fleeting as to be virtually nonexistent. Unfortunately, our case reports of such psychotherapy tend to be chivalric legends, replete with knights and dragons and soothsayers. In view of the difficulties, it is no wonder that they concern themselves with romantic accounts of those rare moments which do seem both lively and comprehensible. And no wonder these moments so often become, in retrospect, a prescriptive exercise in apologetics, taking on the quality of the full-gospel mission: as repentant sinners we announce the miraculous illumination that has possessed us, while the patient, as congregation, shouts "Amen." The conventional scientific prose in which these annunciations are made disguises, but cannot really conceal, the pathos of two maddened human beings clutching at each other, whatever the pretext.

But what of the weeks, months, years, when these two sit together for an hour a day, immersed in a silence broken only by obscure mouthings or posturings conveying no secure meaning; or by earnest professional adjurations that draw no response? How much easier it would be during these desolate periods to abandon what must often seem a bitter mockery of relationship. But the patient has no choice, being captive to his illness and to the explicit rules of the institution. Nor does the therapist have much choice, at least if he is conscientious. Although he is more captive to his conscience than to the institution, conscience obliges him to agree with the unwritten assumption that his mere physical presence each day is necessarily preferable to his absence. Thus does it happen that two people "do time" together under circumstances which, could they be manufactured, would provide the police state with a frightening new torture.

With another kind of patient, the therapist might take refuge in his own thoughts. His silence might pass for that mirrorlike impassivity that is still considered a virtue in the treatment of neurosis. But with a schizophrenic, he has no such refuge. To deprive the patient of ordinary social responsiveness might drive him further from his fragmentary gestures toward his fellows. And silence faced with silence would be arbitrary, if not cruel. Because he knows this, the therapist finds his own silence a heavy burden. He is continually on guard against the double danger of silence and the fear of silence, which he knows can easily sour into a clotted self-consciousness to be relieved at any cost.

At the same moment, perhaps, he is treading another tight-rope between two other dangers. If he fails to grasp the patient's meaning, should he say so frankly or should he temporize? He knows that frankness here, although it will avoid the dangers of empty reassurance, may actually serve his scientific ideal more than his patient—his vanity more than his therapy. And regardless of the solace to be found in scientific caution, he is unhappily aware that a mere affirmation of his own incomprehension is no confirmation of the patient, unless one can be said to confirm another in his estrangement from humanity.

But the therapist cannot afford to hang in indecision: he knows that even the wrong approach is better than none. And so, carefully disclaiming the relevance of what he is about to say, he may now muse or soliloquize aloud to his silent partner in a manner that approaches free association. Or, if he has exhausted his capacity for monologue, he may try reading to the patient. Here he wisely selects some reading matter that, if it does not provoke any response from the patient, will at least be stimulating enough to dull his own self-consciousness. And, if all these substitutes for conversation fail, then he may suggest some shared activity such as a walk about the hospital grounds—which may indeed offer a kind of companionship that goes beyond the limited motives contained in therapy.

Needless to say, no therapist glides rationally from one device to another. And at this point I ought to make it clear that my purpose is not to attack the general theories underlying the kind of treatment I am describing. Whatever criticisms can be made of the details of these theories, I believe they have proved their success in treatment. Moreover, for the therapist himself, these theories often provide his sole support in under-going an experience—I had almost said a "treatment"—that would otherwise be more than human flesh could bear. Considering the grueling nature of this experience and the kind of constancy and courage it demands, it is not surprising if the therapist is driven awkwardly and sometimes blindly by the emptiness of which he is a part. And as he is driven from one expedient to another without success, there will always be moments of extremity when despair forces him to find reasons for abandoning the project altogether. If he succeeds, the reason may be sufficient to persuade his colleagues, himself, and perhaps the patient too. More often he fails even to persuade the others, let alone himself, so that he must return. As the impasse deepens and widens, very little can often be exalted into much: the smallest flicker of humanity, in gesture or grimace, may literally be celebrated as a banquet ending a long fast. Within and without the therapeutic room, the temptation is always present to discover some meaning, that may or may not exist, and thence perhaps to derive the wrong prescription.

When faced with the inevitable despair, which I am suggesting must sooner or later overtake the conscientious therapist, it will not matter how indomitable or inventive may be his efforts to keep going: he cannot hope that his despair will be entirely unnoticed by his patient. Although perceptiveness may be severely impaired in the schizophrenic, the therapist knows that it can never be extinguished—a knowledge that may, in fact, add the final straw to his desolation. What I would suggest here is a possibility that may, since it has been overlooked, offer some truth as well as solace. To the extent that the therapist becomes "present" for his patient, that patient is capable of pity for his friend's distress.

If nothing has been said about the role of pity in treatment, it is because the word is associated partly with thoughts of condescension and partly with those uncomfortable sensations we call "anxiety." It is true that another's misfortune may arouse fear, as well as self-congratulation; but it may also arouse pity. I do not mean sympathy; I mean an actual sensation of pain or grief awakened by another. Thus, everything would depend on the name we give to these sensations. If we call them anxiety, then the thought of arousing further anxiety in the patient can only drive us deeper into our own despair. Add to that the fear of condescension—or worse yet, of arousing condescension in our patients—and we can see that the word "pity" has formidable barriers surrounding it. Nevertheless, *pietas* is an irreplaceable and noble word which, like *caritas* or charity, has been spoiled for us by corruption and abuse. Certainly we cannot replace it with "anxiety," while "sympathy" denotes a mild and vague benevolence that is far removed from love or pity. Once we get past these verbal barriers, then we can consider two possibilities: first, that some pity is unavoidable, even in the therapeutic session, and, second, that it may have some unique value.

I believe that it is quite possible that a patient who has long refused some medical treatment offered to him for his health, because it is good for him, may finally consent to it out of pity. To forestall an obvious objection, I mean unsolicited pity, caused by another's real despair. I do not mean devices reminiscent of Mother's "Take your medicine, dear, for my sake." On the contrary, if pity is achieved, it will be in spite of all solicitations. Pity is a rare and fleeting virtue whose essence is freedom: to be freely given, it must remain unsought or accidental, even fought against.

With this understood, let me examine the suggestion: that a patient may, out of pity, undertake therapeutic efforts, which, although clearly beneficial to himself, have as their primary motive the assuaging of another's pain. In response to the therapist's despair, in other words, the patient will often try to confirm the therapist's image of himself as therapist. And insofar as the therapist is sincerely dedicated to his work —paradoxically, just because he is so dedicated—this will also have the effect of confirming him as a fellow human being. (Once again there is an awesome split between the "human" and the "scientific.")

As I said above, what is done out of pity must be sharply

distinguished from the spurious recoveries that are often attempted either out of flattery or submissiveness, in response to the therapist's vanity or ambition. Pity demands an imagining of the other's particular pain to the degree that the pain is experienced as one's own. In therapy, the paradox is inescapable that the man who is incapable of arousing pity will find it hard to help another.

All this means is that the therapist must be capable of feeling real despair, on another's behalf as well as—and I would stress the fact that we are not supermen—on his own. In addition to the more strenuous virtues of courage and dedication, then, the therapist must be highly endowed with imagination and perceptiveness: capable of imagining his own distress as well as the other's. If we think of the most effective therapists we have known, we can see that when all these qualities are combined to a high degree, they may give rise to a further quality that is perhaps the final secret of the therapeutic success. It is a quality that may take the form of pride, but also of heroism: it is what makes the therapist fight against his own despair and take valiant measures to conceal his weakness. Since these struggles reveal a quality of courage which is universally admired, I think we must assume that it can arouse sympathy and admiration in the patient, just as it does in others. By authenticating the despair, it makes pity possible. And, if we imagine such a powerful emotion as pity being aroused in the patient, we can see that for that moment, at least, he has ceased to be schizophrenic.

If such moments occur more frequently in the treatment of psychosis than of neurosis, it is not, I believe, because schizophrenics are more capable of pity. On the contrary, although the neurotic is far more capable of feeling pity, he is also capable, like the therapist himself, of more intellectual control and criticism. Those emotions that seem to him irrelevant will either be aborted, or they will receive some more acceptable name than pity. But the chief reason is that therapeutic sessions with the relatively controlled and civilized people called "neurotic" simply do not give rise to such overwhelming despair as may evoke pity. There is ample room for both to confirm and be confirmed. And here we can no longer blink the fact that, human nature being what it is, the man who pours out his spiritual energy in confirming others will need more, and not less, confirmation of himself.

If we compare the therapist's job with supposedly more arduous or unrewarding jobs—not so much the medical missionary in the jungle as the man on the assembly line—one difference becomes striking. In a factory, one's body may be chained to one spot, but his thoughts are free: the manual worker may spend his whole day applauding himself in daydream if he chooses. The therapist lacks that freedom, just as he lacks the usual methods for deceiving himself: call them dishonest, childish, or neurotic. Although I would not minimize the awful predicament of the schizophrenic, his illness does operate mercifully to spare him the full realization of his misery. Those who befriend him lack such protection.

This makes the therapist unusually dependent on the confirmation he can get from friends and family, and especially from colleagues. And although I do not suggest that his colleagues will underestimate the need for confirmation, I do think we have added one or two unnecessary burdens to the load—not deliberately, as though a medical missionary were to take up wearing a hair shirt—but out of inertia, as though we had inherited a hair shirt we have not bothered to remove. There is first the concealed ideal of moral perfection that operates only when it is not acknowledged. Implicit in Western society is the ideal of a teacher or healer who confirms others without needing confirmation for himself. Second, there is the modern psychological vocabulary of motive that so readily translates itself into terms of moral character and behavior and is notorious for the ease with which it can be exploited for character assassination. Finally, there are certain occupational hazards, vested interests of the profession, that may add needless burdens.

What happens when the despairing therapist turns for confirmation to his colleagues? To imagine the situation at its best: although offering sympathy, the colleagues will not, of course, confirm despair or hopelessness. They will look for hope—that is to say, for meaning; they will point out the moments when the therapist has gone astray. On the assumption that every situation is both meaningful and manageable, had one but the "psychological freedom" to control it, they will gently show him where he has failed his calling or his patient. And this, of course, is reassuring. Since anything is preferable to meaninglessness, the therapist longs to find some point at which he may accuse himself of moral guilt or of a failure of imagination.

On the other hand, considering the difficulties of human communication in general, it is doubtful that a therapist faced with total chaos or lack of meaning will succeed in conveying this particular chaos with any accuracy to his colleagues. Indeed, success here depends on his ability to translate chaos into some familiar meaning. Even the greatest artist would find it hard to represent chaos, and insofar as he succeeded, the more urgent would become one's need to fill it in with meaning. The more chaotic the treatment situation, then, the faster do we rush in with explanations and prescriptions. Now here I am not worrying about the danger to the patient; it is in the nature of our calling, as with those who deal with children, that we must always make the best of hasty diagnoses and inadequate prescriptions, as preferable to none at all. We are always having either to trust the Lord or to put our faith in the sturdiness of human nature. I am thinking rather of the effect upon the therapist. The only confirmation he can get from his colleagues will confirm him in his dedication or his calling: it will supply the meanings and reinforce the existing theories by which his efforts are supported.

Even were the colleagues willing to listen to a long confessional, or to provide absolution at the end, what is he able to confess? Not the real despair, caused by the real absence of meaning and response; not his real situation, of being too long immersed in this void of meaning. He can only confess whatever shape or order can be fashioned out of chaos— whatever moral guilt or failure his imagination can contrive. Sometimes the guilt arrives first, as an ever-present, indeed a universal condition of the human; then guilt, turning backward, can easily supply some missing cry of need, some failure to respond. But here it is not the imperfection of man, set against perfection, that arouses moral guilt. Guilt is welcomed simply as a meaning, one of the handiest of familiar meanings, to get us out of chaos.[21]

I have been discussing two well-known hazards of the profession: first, the temptation toward both omniscience and perfection, and, second, the opposite—the too-ready cry of *mea culpa* that follows on the discovery of one's own fallibility and imperfection. But I have tried to suggest how irrelevant in the treatment of schizophrenia the *mea culpa* may become— how impotent to describe a plight that must approach uniqueness. Certainly no man has been more guiltless than one who kneels at the very edge of nothingness, hoping to save a fallen

[21] Given his real situation, and the general difficulty of "imagining the real," the therapist will not, of course, achieve a greater accuracy with the help of a tape machine or movie camera. The same difficulties are merely transferred to a medium less trustworthy, and far less comprehensive, than memory. On top of such valid ideals, however impossible, as moral perfection and total omniscience, the modern techniques have only added a silly reduction of omniscience to the capacity of a machine—that is, to such facts as may be recorded and preserved intact, purified of meaning or interpretation, in some mechanical vaults of memory.

175

stranger. To remain in this posture for days and weeks and even years, calling oneself guilty in order to stave off hopelessness—surely this is no easy brand of fellowship. And the colleagues surrounding one, all bent in the same posture: they may have a helping hand to spare each other, but they will not have time to applaud themselves as heroes. Like any rescue crew, they are more apt to snap irritably at each other, "Get a grip on yourself, man—that rope is slipping."

So perhaps it is not only the technical vocabulary, but the work itself that may explain a phenomenon puzzling and often shocking to the uninitiated. I mean the irritable and occasionally savage criticism of technique which one member of a rescue crew may turn upon another. It is for a common good, after all, that self-criticism should be brutally frank and also limited to technique. For it is on the strength and dexterity of each hand that the whole enterprise is literally hanging. And it would be neither possible nor helpful for the team to support a failing member by confirming his despair. In fact, the closer he comes to hopelessness, and the more he succeeds in conveying this to his fellows, the faster they will turn on him with the full resources of their technical vocabulary. And, as I have mentioned, the psycoanalytic vocabulary is probably unique for the ease with which it may be exploited for attack.

If, to avoid despair, the therapist must either attack himself or be attacked for moral failure, then a circle is created by which the attack adds further to despair. If this is unavoidable in our profession, then we must resign ourselves. But insofar as we can find needless burdens arising not so much from human weakness as from simple intellectual errors, then the situation looks more hopeful. It is unnecessary, for example, to add a fear of despair to our other burdens, when despair may be called the honorable stigma of our calling. This can be seen as an error of logic, by which a superhuman strength or omnipotence is added to our other professional qualifications, and any human weakness becomes another moral sin. But chiefly, I think this fear comes less from error than from the necessary modesty of all heroic undertakings: to admit the possibility of despair is also to admit the possibility of failure.

Let me return for a moment to the less heroic hazards that mine the fields of great exploits. If it is a general hazard of the profession that our case reports should be chivalric legends, homiletic exercises, and large annunciations of the small success, we can understand why this should be. Even the relatively easy sessions with neurosis may be discouraging enough to tempt us with mirages. It is then that we see large vistas opening up: visions of some larger meaning, expanded out of very little. With psychosis, not only are meanings elusive and discouragements ten times multiplied, but a dimension of terror is added to our existence, as we learn to live with the insane possibility—which is, after all, one of the facts of madness—that meaning itself can be the mirage. To avoid this insanity, we grasp at every possibility of meaning as though it were the staunchest fact.

One result of this is a fever, sparing none of us, that might be called an *obsessive anecdotalism* around the subject of therapy. The trouble with these anecdotes is not that they are boring or pointless; on the contrary, they have too much point. Like the short short-story in a magazine, episodes in treatment come to be reported as though they were tidy slices of life: compact, oversimplified, and contrived in their denouement. And, as the anecdotes become obsessive, haunting the therapist's imagination, they may overflow the hospital situation to include, in addition to his colleagues, his friends, his family, and even his publications. Unlike the traumatic nightmare that returns vainly each night to the scene of disaster, such obsessive anecdotalism is a waking nightmare, no less troubling because it is successful in its outcome. And equally troubling, of course, are those anecdotes that seek to escape the charge of immodesty by stressing some conspicuous failure of the therapist, which is then corrected by the patient. In either case, it is the anecdote that fails its purpose. I am not suggesting that the therapist's memory has falsified the facts, but only that the human mind cannot deal with chaos and disorder: memory cannot record it. Although the anecdote is clearly the wrong genre for recording the experience of therapy, it arises from no aesthetic or myth-making impulse, but quite the reverse. There is such a thing as a need for facts, events—for something to happen, if only in our heads—which, in the treatment of schizophrenia, has been drastically and continually thwarted.

The danger is obvious, both for the therapist himself and for the whole of psychotherapy. Not only is the therapist, at the height of his fever, unable to seek confirmation of himself as he is or would be, and forced instead to look for mere congratulation; but, more important, a treatment seen and reported in these anecdotal terms will come to be practiced in these terms. And any therapist who enters on his life with a schizophrenic expecting it to resemble the case reports is doomed, if not to premature despair, at least to more discouragement than necessary.

Closely connected with the need for meaning is the problem of identity, which I would mention now as a final hazard. Since a crucial goal of treatment is the development or, in some cases, the acquisition of an identity, it is inevitable that the patient will at some stage begin to borrow his identity from the therapist. Indeed, the recovering patient will often appear to the outsider to be more artifice than person: a rag bag of oddly assorted scraps of theory, manner, and language, filched mainly from the therapist. Now it would be manifestly unfair to conclude from this that the therapist was using some hypnotic method, or that the cure is even more inauthentic than the disease. But without denying that authoritarian methods do exist, most of us have gone to the opposite extreme—especially if we have succumbed to that belief, usually acquired during our student days, that a good scientist would never inflict any of his own values on his patient or student.

If we therefore accuse ourselves of inflicting a pseudo-identity on the patient, this becomes another needless burden, as pointless as for parents to accuse themselves of setting an example for their children. With schizophrenics, of course, we count ourselves lucky if they consent to borrow anything at all from their surroundings. But in many other cases where identity is shadowy—in much so-called hysteria, for example—we are less apt to inflict a pseudo-identity on the patient than to have one inflicted on us. In fact, the therapist is so often forced, against his better judgment, to play the role of oracle or all-knowing authority that I wonder to what extent we have developed our vocabulary of transference and counter-transference, of father-surrogates and mother-surrogates, in order to account for this phenomenon.

Once we recover from the delusion that psychology is an exact science, or that scientists do not have values, then it is easier to help the patient through these supposedly inauthentic stages of his recovery. For one thing, we are more willing to admit that what has to be recovered from is not only the disease, but also the treatment. And, while we generally leave it up to the patient to recover from us, so to speak, as best he can, there is no reason why we should not try to help him through this period of recovery, during which he tries to decide just which of our values should be kept and which discarded. For it is upon this critical process of selection that the final phase of recovery will depend, whether it occurs during or after treatment.

If such intellectual processes are generally regarded as the province of pedagogy rather than of therapy, this may be partly because they do admittedly have less to do with interpersonal relations than with some solitary exercise of reasoning and judgment—less to do with dialogue, in other words, than with monologue. And this brings me to the last point I want to make. It has to do with monologue—not at the expense of dialogue or relationship, but as one of the necessary movements in dialogue. There is a growing tendency in modern times—not only among psychotherapists—to let our concern with the interpersonal overshadow certain other values that are personal or solitary in character.

I mentioned above that a good therapist must be able to imagine his own despair, as well as the patient's. For the task of "imagining the real" must include oneself, just as it includes those moments in which the other person cannot be vividly present to us. Although the capacity to experience another's distress as though it were our own may be valued as the highest human capacity, it is not the only form of knowledge. Nor is it apt to be highly developed among those who spend all their waking moments in converse with their fellows. As an example of monologue, one may think of a teacher-student relationship, and draw certain analogies to the doctor-patient relation. Despite the modern tendency to regard all teaching relationships as primarily interpersonal in character, it is obvious that a teacher's primary dedication must be not to his students but to his subject matter. Were this not so, teaching would consist only of those romantic relations, based on vanity or power, which the psychotherapist has learned to call "transference" situations.

Instead, a good teacher's initial address to his students will be monologic, very much like the initial address of an author to his reader. The reader must sit silent as the author has his lengthy say. Characters and plot and style may create the illusion that this is not a single man speaking, but so it is with any genuinely imagined monologue. As his interest quickens, the reader—or the student—comes to have a lively consort not with the author, not with the teacher in his person, but only with the work at hand. Obviously any student who spent his time in class thinking only about the teacher's personal life, or imagining his private thoughts and feelings, would not be learning much. And the same is true of a reader, for it is only after a prolonged acquaintance with an author that the man himself will begin to emerge somewhat from his work. Any premature effort to detach him—to imagine what he himself is wishing, feeling, perceiving, thinking—would be as self-defeating in the arts as it would be destructive of any other educative process. Although teacher and student may both confirm and be confirmed in their mutual endeavor, this process must remain both indirect and secondary to the goal of learning. True dialogue here, as with all collective efforts, would be concerned not with the other person, but with a mutual dedication to the same end.

In Buber's dialogic philosophy, as in the usual psychology of interpersonal relations, the concept of monologue carries a pejorative meaning, signifying a failure in discourse. In this sense, the obsessive anecdotalism mentioned earlier would be an example of monology. Yet, in a deeper sense, there are crucial moments for man when his utterance must be mono-logic—moments when the actuality of other men must recede from his awareness. It might be argued that Buber, unlike Kierkegaard, almost out of an excess of virtue, often appears too consummatory in his view of human relations. But, on the other hand, he has written—in a context that has little to do with imagining the other: "The origin of all conflict between me and my fellowmen is that I do not say what I mean, and that I do not do what I say."[22] And in words reminiscent of Kierkegaard: "Every single man is a new thing in the world, and is called upon to fulfill his particularity in this world. . . .

[22] Martin Buber, *The Way of Man* (Greenwich, Conn.: Seabury Press, 1950), p. 32.

Mankind's great chance lies precisely in the unlikeness of men, in the unlikeness of their qualities and inclinations."[23]

In saying what he means, what he alone means, man seeks to express his own being or the being he would become. Such expressions in no way confirm the other in his particularity. If confirmation can be said to exist at all, it is of general nature: in affirming my own unlikeness, I may be confirming yours, or asserting the particularity of all men. In that "whole earth" that "is our hospital," dialogue must include general statements about dialogue, just as it must include our most desolate or solitary monologues.

In this earthly "hospital," I have spoken of the patient's need to recover from his treatment. But there is a deeper sense in which the cure may be implicit in the disease. As Freud taught long ago, there is some health in every symptom; or, "to be restored, our sickness must grow worse." And this holds true, not only for the patient, but for that therapeutic despair that is, after all, a collaboration between two people. If there are moments when it seems that "our only health is the disease," and we must "obey the dying nurse whose constant care is not to please but to remind of our, and Adam's curse," these are not inauthentic moments. On the contrary, it is when we stand stripped of every artifice and prop, every technical support of our profession, that we are closest to reality. And if it is only then, in the moment of extremity, that we approach genuine dialogue, genuine confirmation—the lack of which has driven us to this despair—so we may find the remedy concealed in the disease. It may be that only in such moments do we approach reality at all. It may be that at such moments the patient, too, is obeying such deep and elementary needs that it would be gratuitous to speak of pity and despair. But however that may be, it is only when the therapist has exhausted every conceivable device for reaching his patient that

23 *Ibid.,* p. 17.

he may, from the very heart of his despair, cry out with his entire being, as if to his Maker. Such a cry is as far from dialogue or confirmation as it is from love or sympathy; any response awakened by it will be a response to pain and loneliness. In Kierkegaard's words:

One must really have suffered very much in the world, and have been very unfortunate before there can be any talk of beginning to love one's neighbor. It is only in dying to the joys and happiness of the world in self-denial that the neighbor comes into existence. One cannot therefore accuse the immediate person of not loving his neighbor, because he is too happy for the "neighbor" to exist for him. No one who clings to earthly life loves his neighbor, that is to say his neighbor does not exist for him.[24]

Although such "dying to the world" is not readily or often chosen, especially nowadays, there is no denying that much loneliness and suffering can still be imposed through one's chosen profession. And unless this is to be a useless form of suffering, a total waste of spirit, we must learn how to name and accept our own despair.

[24] Sören Kierkegaard, *The Journals of Kierkegaard*, edited and translated by Alexander Dru (London: Oxford University Press, 1938), p. 219.

9

SCHIZOPHRENIA
AND THE MAD
PSYCHOTHERAPIST

In Chapter 8, I attempted to describe the peculiar and painful nature of the therapeutic life with schizophrenia—its emptiness, meaninglessness, lack of confirmation—in short, the circumstances that lead to a particular despair on the part of the therapist and that may subsequently evoke in the patient a response of pity for his doctor's plight. I suggested further that such pity might very well lead the patient to assuage the therapist's anguish through therapeutic movements intended to confirm the therapist as therapist. It seemed to me then, as it seems to me now, that despair is more or less intrinsic to the therapeutic life with schizophrenia and that such despair, moreover, if acknowledged rather than disowned, if contended with rather than evaded, *might* (the word is important) have a salutary effect on therapy.

My aim in this chapter is to examine what happens, especially to the therapist himself, when this despair is *not* acknowledged, not contended with.

By and large, the response of my colleagues to the earlier paper was one of agreement, although several older therapists, some exceptionally capable in their work, were not persuaded by my argument, feeling that my account of the agonies of therapy was both overdrawn and unfaithful to their own experience.

And, while I was working on the paper and was absorbed with schizophrenia and the hazards of ministering to it, I became aware that a number of younger therapists, each with several years' experience treating schizophrenia, were seeking, in one way or another, to take their leave of this area of psychiatry. The reasons they contrived for abandoning their work with schizophrenics were various, but I began gradually to suspect that underlying all their logic and detachment, their talk of the value of varied clinical experience, of opportunities elsewhere, of a yearning for private practice was a vague and brooding, and unspoken, apprehension that their sanity was at stake. In this apprehension, they were often joined by their wives, who also felt vaguely troubled by subtle changes in their husbands. Although they had difficulty describing this alteration, they seemed to have no doubt that it constituted an unhappy development. Even when nagged or beseeched by their husbands for reassurance, these wives were unwilling or unable to consider the changes they observed as part of a decent maturation of character. I am trying as carefully as possible to avoid being clinical. Clinical categorizing here would be as inappropriate to our purposes of describing and understanding as clinical self-scrutiny was inadequate to the perplexing and ominous restlessness these younger therapists found themselves caught up in. Neither they nor their wives worried that they might fall victim to a particular clinical disorder, least of all schizophrenia. If they feared for their sanity, it was in a private, unprofessional way; they wondered to what degree they were becoming what they were not, or—

with equal relevance—to what degree they were not becoming what they were.

At any rate, the objections raised by some of my older friends to my paper on therapeutic despair, as well as the uneasiness and concern of these younger men, have prompted me to reconsider my own experience in this area. For a period of over twenty years that includes working with schizophrenics, as well as those young doctors who spend their days treating schizophrenic patients, I have also had the good fortune to know and to be instructed by several very great therapists, therapists with grave theoretical differences, but sharing nevertheless that power sometimes called "charisma," which the dictionary defines as: "a grace, as a miraculously given power of healing, or of speaking with tongues, or of prophesying, etc., attributed to some of the early Christians." Then, too, I have had a passing acquaintance with those occasional, ragged, even disreputable healers who seem to burst full-blown, apparently with little preparation, into the world of schizophrenia, brandishing their therapeutic powers with a flourish that far exceeds their theoretical accomplishments. Their period of therapeutic vitality is usually comparatively brief, and their subsequent course or fate, disagreeable. In short then, as I looked about me at three different groups of therapists— the young, the old, and the vagabonds—I could not escape concluding, allowing for certain remarkable exceptions, that the hazards are indeed serious for those who choose to devote their professional lives to the treatment of schizophrenia.

I sometimes wonder what impression the hospital world of schizophrenia—for example, a sanitarium devoted exclusively or primarily to schizophrenic patients—might make on someone who happened into it without advance explanation or preparation. His first thought, one he would quickly correct, would be that it was difficult to tell the doctors from the patients. But, as soon as he dismissed this notion—in spite of conceits to the contrary it is not a difficult distinction—I suspect that, as he observed the therapists in ordinary conversation and listened to them in meeting, it might strike him that no word but theatrical or histrionic could do descriptive justice to their extraordinary manner. He would have to conclude that, for reasons mysterious to himself, these therapists had apparently abandoned what must once have been their more usual habits of expression in favor of some more florid and declamatory style—a style that appeared to transcend style, elevating mere form or manner to substance itself.

At this point, let me describe an incident from the therapeutic practice of a friend—one of the most distinguished therapists of schizophrenia in modern times. The incident is not especially unusual and may, therefore, suggest the flavor of the life within an institution devoted to the treatment of schizophrenia, as it might appear to an outsider.

My friend the therapist had been treating a schizophrenic young man for about a year and a half. The therapy had had its ordinary portion of difficulty, impasse, silence, violence, and the like, but, at the time of this incident, seemed to be moving along satisfactorily. My friend owned a fountain pen of which he was very fond. It was an excellent pen, valuable, distinctive in appearance, and reliable. Not only did it give him pleasure on all these counts, but it also had personal significance for him, having been a birthday gift from his father. My friend used this pen constantly, carrying it with him in his breast pocket wherever he went. Somehow, in the course of a therapeutic session, the pen came to the attention of the patient, who seemed to admire it. He watched attentively as my friend used it to make notes, then hesitantly reached his own hand toward it. Noticing this gesture, the therapist, instead of returning the pen to his pocket, put it into his patient's hand and said, "Pretty, isn't it? Do you want to try it out?" The patient slowly fondled the pen, then suddenly unscrewed the cap and fell to making marks on a sheet of paper the therapist had placed before him. Totally absorbed, he hunched over his work, manipulating the pen with care and deliberation. Although solemn and silent, as was customary, he seemed to be enjoying himself. Heartened by this responsiveness—if only to his fountain pen—and reluctant to ignore any opportunity for relation, the therapist said, "Look, how would you like to keep the pen until tomorrow? Maybe you could write a letter with it tonight. You can bring it back to me at our hour tomorrow." The patient stopped marking the paper and gazed down at the pen, then up at the ceiling, then out the window, and finally into the therapist's face. "Thank you," he said. The remainder of the hour went very well.

The following therapeutic session came and went without mention of the pen. And the following one. And the one after that. And then several more. At last, after some weeks had passed, my friend inquired politely about his pen and mentioned how convenient it would be to have it back again. The patient said nothing, but appeared to have heard the therapist's remarks. A few more therapeutic hours passed with no sign or mention of the pen, and finally one day my friend said, "I don't want to press you about this, but the matter of my fountain pen is increasingly on my mind. I'm sure I didn't mention it to you at the time you borrowed it, but that pen means a great deal to me. I realize this may be sheer childishness on my part, but, you see, it was a present from my father, a little while before he died, as a matter of fact, and I'm very attached to it. Of course, I could easily just buy myself another pen, or use a pencil, and forget the whole thing. But, as I've explained, I'm especially fond of that particular pen. This may all seem quite silly to you, but surely you know how people sometimes become devoted to certain objects. . . . Well, maybe it *is* silly, but the fact remains that I *am* devoted to that pen, and I'd appreciate very much having it back. So, would

188

you please bring it along with you next time?" There was no answer, but my friend assumed he had made his point and that it had registered. However, the fountain pen failed to appear at the next interview, or the next, or the next. A few sessions later my friend introduced the subject still another time. "About my pen. . . . You've had it six weeks now. Don't you think that's about long enough to keep a borrowed fountain pen? I've explained it all very carefully to you—why I'm anxious to have it back, and so forth. Now, please don't fail to bring the pen with you tomorrow."

And, two meetings later, "My patience is wearing thin. I mean to have that pen, and I don't want any more foolishness about it. Time after time I've asked you gently and politely to return it; I've explained how I feel about it, and why I insist on having it back, and all this has produced no result whatever. You don't return it, you won't discuss it. Now what the hell is all this about? Can you tell me that?" After a long silence the patient murmured, "It's lost." "It's *what?* What do you mean *lost?*" No answer. "Are you trying to tell me that you no longer have my fountain pen? You don't have it with you? It's not in your room? In other words, it's *gone?*" Again the patient made no answer; in fact, he remained absolutely silent throughout the rest of the hour, while the therapist thundered at him and stomped about the office.

The interview concluded on this uncordial note, and the patient returned to his room. Immediately the therapist summoned two hospital attendants, and the three of them marched off toward the ward where the patient lived. When they reached his room, the therapist gave a curt order, and the attendants flung wide the door, bounded inside, and in a matter of seconds had the startled young man on his back, pinned to the floor. My friend then entered the room, and without taking the least notice of his gasping and astonished patient, made a rapid but efficient search for his pen. He found it in the drawer of the desk. He picked it up, regarded it a moment, glanced briefly at his pinioned patient while he jabbed the pen into his breast pocket, then wheeled about and stalked from the room. As he was making his exit the patient raised his head from the floor and shouted past the attendants toward his retreating therapist, "My God, what a madhouse! All this fuss about one little fountain pen!"

I am at pains to point out that my friend is a courteous, civilized person, whose normal manner—at least among friends —is gracious and reserved and ironic. Ordinarily, he is simply not given to such carrying on as I have described. It would be more characteristic, in such a circumstance, for him to acknowledge that the problem of the borrowed-pen-gone-astray is the inevitable concern of anyone who has—and lends— cherished possessions, and, after polite efforts to retrieve some item had failed, he would, without undue commotion, replace it. This display over his patient's failure, or refusal, to return his pen is curiously uncharacteristic and might even be said to be enacted somewhat larger than life. But we must be careful with our interpretations at this point. My friend is no method actor, who will facetiously describe to his wife during dinner the experimental situation he engaged in with his patient, reenacting his gestures and lines for her amusement. At no time, either while with his patient or when recounting the incident to his wife, does the therapist imagine himself to be *acting* at all. In talking with his wife, he will declare, quite sincerely, that his exasperating patient provoked him beyond all human endurance, driving him to take the measures he took. The one thing about the incident that would surely strike an observer will just as surely escape the attention of the therapist himself, namely, that this collision of wills has been shockingly naked, clothed by none of the artifices that usually conceal willfulness. If my friend has been theatrical, his theatricality has been effective enough to deceive himself. He may be ruthless in rooting out his motives for this violent action; he will call them "countertransference," which will enable him, by convicting himself of a vanity that led him to offer the pen in the first place, to seize full psychological responsibility for the whole encounter. Still, he will not be troubled by the quality and scope of his performance, nor is he likely to consider the possibility that the whole affair could be a fictitious alternative for some real moral dilemma confronting him and his patient. As a matter of fact, once he has thrashed out his motives—alone or, more commonly, with the assistance of his wife or a colleague—he may decide his handling of this incident has been direct, even courageous. Naturally, to come to this conclusion he will have to forget that the hospital situation stacks the deck in his favor; without a tremor, bravely, and in full view of the audience, he has shot the villain with a stage revolver loaded with blank cartridges.

Let me mention another incident, this one from the practice of the late Dr. Frieda Fromm-Reichmann, one of the most gifted people to work with schizophrenia.

Dr. Fromm-Reichmann was seeing an extremely disabled young man who had been schizophrenic for years. He was habitually dirty and disheveled; he rarely spoke and even more rarely achieved much coherence in what little speech he did produce. Without question, therapeutic work with this patient was a grim business, affording scant hope, little satisfaction, and few of even those fleeting rewards so precious to the therapist who specializes in the treatment of schizophrenia. One day, during a therapeutic hour, as this patient (mute, as usual) was sitting with Dr. Fromm-Reichmann in her office, she noticed that he was fingering his genitals with one hand that was crammed deep into the pocket of his trousers. It was also plain to her that he had an erection. She pondered this situation for a moment, then said to him, "If it will make you feel any better, please go ahead." Whereupon the young man unzipped his fly and proceeded to masturbate, while Dr. Fromm-Reichmann sat quietly across from him, her eyes down, her hands clasped in her lap.

Anyone who knew Dr. Fromm-Reichmann at all knew that she was a well-brought-up, refined, upper middle-class, German Jewish lady. During Georg Groddeck's last years, prior to his commitment to an institution, she performed the offices of his hostess with fastidious skill. Once or twice a year, she helped Groddeck to assemble at his estate a group of distinguished European psychiatrists. It was her duty to arrange for food and wine and cigars and in general to put these guests (many of whom did not know one another) at their ease, to ensure a comfortable social atmosphere out of which might come the sort of conversation Groddeck wished about matters psychoanalytic. Once the group had gathered, following all her work of arrangement and preparation, she was required, as the only woman present, to assist in the setting of the scene and in the maintenance of the appropriate tone to the occasion, but always without calling attention either to her assistance or to the novelty of her presence. But, of course, it might happen that in the consideration of some question of feminine psychology, Groddeck would suddenly turn to her and say, "Frieda, we men cannot really know about these things. As a woman, Frieda, you must instruct us." At such moments, I am sure, she was more than rewarded for the physical and emotional labor of these occasions, not to mention the irritations involved in dealing with a person as crotchety and difficult as Groddeck became in his later years.

Dr. Fromm-Reichmann was always a marvelous hostess, and something of her quality as hostess appears in the incident I have recounted about her and the mute young man who was encouraged to masturbate if it would help him to feel more comfortable. But I doubt that as this man sat masturbating in her quiet office, full of tasteful mementoes of her European past, she found much resemblance to her life as Groddeck's hostess. To some extent a hostess resembles an actress, in that she plays a role (in this case, one of amiability toward a group she may not know); she is not required to believe that her role is anything more than a role. As with an actress, believability is central to the effectiveness of the performance, but in order that it be achieved, actual personal sincerity—in regard to the scene itself—is unnecessary, if not irrelevant. In therapeutic encounters, on the other hand, the therapist's actual personal sincerity is considered absolutely essential to the occasion. I think that as Dr. Fromm-Reichmann described this incident with the mute and masturbating young man at a staff conference, she might well have blamed herself for some awkwardness in her invitation, and she would have been quick to acknowledge any erotic titillation she experienced. But she would have resisted the suggestion that there was anything unusual about her behavior, that while committed, in full sincerity, to her duties as psychotherapist she had suddenly found herself enacting the role of hostess. Her private conviction, I suspect, would have been, as in our previous example, that there was something real, something "down-to-earth" about this incident.

It does not actually matter if the part an actor plays is not really relevant to his life, because he knows (I am speaking ideally, of course) that he is playing a part. The therapist, however, is not granted such distance; he may be theatrical, but he is not playing a part. (Unlike the actor, he may believe what he will or will what he believes.) As he comes to believe in the reality of these overblown therapeutic encounters, so rich in the materials of strife and sexuality, it is his ordinary life outside the hospital that may come to appear artificial and pallid. It is not unusual for the therapist, as he settles into his work with schizophrenia, to begin to prefer the company of schizophrenics, even those who are mute. Given the extraordinary difficulty of treating schizophrenia, it might be expected that with experience, status, and income, the older therapist would try to restrict the hours he spends with schizophrenic patients. More often than not, the opposite is the case: he tends to fill more and more of his waking hours with such therapeutic work, and to feel quite bereft and impotent and lonely, when, for reasons of illness or vacation or grants, he is deprived of the schizophrenic's company. I shall return to this unusual preference later.

In telling the story about the therapist and the borrowed pen, I suggested that the whole incident had a quality of being somehow larger than life. But it is not merely the therapeutic encounter which is habitually writ large in this way; something of this quality passes over from the event to the man, and not infrequently the gifted therapists themselves come to be writ large. They begin to resemble certain spectacular personalities—often, but by no means exclusively, actors and show people—in that they no sooner enter a room than they fill it. Room after room after room, differences of setting and occasion mattering not at all, confronted with a room they fill it, in what becomes a characteristic style of their own, yet not predictable—as mere idiosyncrasy of manner is—and flexible enough to adapt itself to any particular situation. Just *how* they accomplish this, time after time, must to some extent remain a mystery; but what we have noted about their therapeutic life may give some clue to this quality of compelling social, or personal, presence, shared by a surprising number of therapists who have spent years in the company of schizophrenics, a quality that seems gradually to unfold to full-flower—quite a *large* flower, usually—in them over the years. Let me be quite clear here: filling a room is not merely —and sometimes not at all—a matter of talking long and loud; even silence may, on occasion, produce a unique resonance, affecting an entire scene. Nor can this capacity be attributed merely to physical manner. Manner is not unimportant, but it is more likely to be the vehicle (or perhaps only the packaging) of the effect than the key to its cause. It is true that *what* is said is usually less important than *how* it is said, but even here both the what and the how tend to vary with the therapist's dramatic feel of the occasion. There is, however, one general statement that we can make about such a man and his manner: what he cannot or will not countenance is distance and—as a result—any real absorption in subject matter. His province is relation: not the relation that may slowly emerge out of content, nor even the relation that may come from a leisurely exchange of personal forthrightness, which always risks alienation as its culmination, when two people strive (with success or without) to reveal themselves to each other. In one way or another, this room-filling therapist manipulates and forces the spell of relation, willfully exploiting whatever personal expedients come to mind.

In order to understand better this connection between will and relation—which I believe to be crucial to our subject—let us remind ourselves of the nature of the therapeutic life with schizophrenia. In Chapter 8 (see especially pages 168–169) I attempted to portray something of the agony of the therapeutic life with schizophrenia that may end in what I have called "the therapeutic despair." But, as some of my older friends have reminded me, despair is not inevitable; in fact, they would prefer to believe such despair is a morbid consequence of this work—as unhealthy, perhaps, as my own preoccupation with the subject.

I would like to suggest that avoiding despair by reducing it to a merely "morbid" or "unhealthy" state of mind—and thus refusing to conceive it as belonging inescapably in some measure to our lives as human beings—may be more malignant than despair itself. (It was Kierkegaard's belief that the worst of all despairs is that in which one does not know he is in despair.) It sometimes happens that despair itself provides the very condition of urgency that brings a man to ask those serious—we might call them tragic—questions about his life and the meaning and measure of his particular humanness. When despair is repudiated, these questions go unasked, and it may be exactly here, in the failure to confront these questions, that there occurs a turning in one's development that is false.

Let us consider again the situation in which the therapist, knowing that even the wrong approach is better than none, may muse or soliloquize aloud to his silent partner. For most therapists who persist in this field, such soliloquizing becomes their principal refuge or solace—or, from their standpoint, the form in which their therapeutic powers find their most vigorous expression. While the schizophrenic may be largely unresponsive to the social event, every therapist holds the premise that the patient hungers for relation at the same time that he lacks the ordinary personal grace that might bring such relation about. Moreover, he fears that should he venture an overture he might, owing to his gross deficiency, increase his estrangement by revealing himself as even more unacceptable than he already appears. Given the schizophrenic's incapacities, not to mention his experience in hypocrisy and betrayal, the overtures of others will seem to him even more dubious than his own. Obviously, such a situation imposes a formidable constraint on what may be said.

How may we characterize this constraint? There is, of course, the fact of inequality between these two people: one is patient, the other, doctor; one is confined, the other, free; one is mad, the other, sane. And this essential inequality must be contended with—validly or invalidly. Equally important is the choice and treatment of subject matter. Of what shall the therapist speak? And in what manner, from what view, to what point? If he were to talk about the daily events of his life, however scrupulously he stripped them of color and meaning and relevance, he would still imply a world in which he lived and worked, a world from which he himself was not estranged. And, aside from the effect on the patient, such a drab recital might very likely be dispiriting to the therapist, so eager himself to make some relational thrust into this seeming vacuum. (I am, of course, taking for granted that he will carefully avoid all those topics that might impinge on the patient's delusional propensities.) Since we may assume with some safety that the therapist himself is not schizophrenic, we will expect that in addition to having a world he lives with*in* rather than with*out*, he is also blessed by affectionate connections with friends and, very possibly, a family as well —all of which, for our present purposes, can be called relation. Unless he is sadistic, frantic, or simply stupid, he is hardly likely to expatiate to his schizophrenic patient over moments of intimacy with friends and family. If he chooses to speak of these people at all, it will probably be in order to emphasize whatever estrangement exists or has existed, seeking to appeal to his patient on the level of a fellow sufferer. The danger here, postponing momentarily the insidious effect this device may have on the therapist himself, is that often, to the patient, such talk about estrangement will serve to invoke intimations of those times when estrangement is (or was) either overcome or absent altogether. To forestall this danger, the therapist, almost without realizing it, may overstate and overgeneralize his case. Not deliberately, of course, since he is not being dishonest, but, in his need to join his patient, he may inventively overextend and exaggerate the oppressiveness of the situation he describes. And, since he is not an actor playing a part, and, more important still, since his own sincerity is essential to his convictions, as well as to the assurance with which he believes he must address his patient, he may succeed in persuading himself that through his work with his patient he has discovered patterns of pathology in himself and in his private life whose significance he had not heretofore appreciated, or perhaps even suspected. This is not the only way certainly, but it is an important way in which the therapist seeks, and often finds, kinship with his patient: discovering (or so he believes) his own schizophrenic possibilities. As he pursues such objectifications of himself and his life and his past, he comes to speak with a clarity about himself as a psychological dynamism that is not only excessive, but that may be quite false. But again, being no actor, he may, as the years in this work roll by, begin to confuse this deterministic construction with himself. And the assembling of this construction is, of course, aided and abetted by the fact that it will seldom, if ever, be challenged or affirmed by the patient. Since determinism itself is not necessarily an evil affair—it may be appropriate or inappropriate, simple or complex—is there anything we can say about the nature of the construction that the therapist contrives to represent himself? By and large, so far as I have been able to tell, regardless of the particular school of psychoanalysis to which he belongs, the therapist comes to view himself as victim, acted upon by forces of nature, society, or family in such a manner or at such an early age as to render him powerless. Whether he finds his victimization during the first six months of his life, when he failed to surpass the "paranoid position" postulated by Melanie Klein, or locates his trauma in the anxious mothering he received, according to Sullivanian theory, or—in modern fashion—discovers the "double bind" in which his parents trapped him; his story will be the familiar one of hero-as-victim irreversibly oppressed by the will of others. "I am this way because . . . ," he announces to his patient as casually as possible, implying that it *is* possible to live this life in spite of devastating victimization. Or, "The mood I inflicted on you yesterday has its explanation in a conflict I have been having with your

198

ward administrator." Or, "My failure to hear you has always been provoked by withdrawal, whether yours or my mother's." Or, "Last Thursday night I had a dream in which I raped you. I tell you this so that you may understand my coolness these last few days." And so on. Such remarks will be regarded, not as acknowledgments of moral limitation, but as manifestations of "countertransference," usually referring to personal attitudes acquired in the past and now inappropriate. We should notice here the easy and translucent clarity of these statements: in vain will we seek here for a hint of mystery, ambiguity, paradox, surprise, or uncertainty. Our visitor to the sanitarium, hearing several such therapists in conference (naturally they speak to one another about themselves in much the same way as to their patients), might, if he were impressionable, briefly believe that he had stumbled on a small band of medical monks, so brutally honest did their confessions seem. But, as he listened further, the utilitarian nature of this seeming candor might soon strike him; he would note that such "countertransference" explanations by and large afforded whatever meaning it seemed possible to provide in a painfully chaotic situation. Of course, he could not help but observe that these confessions were delivered, whether to patients or colleagues, rather cheerfully, unlike his own halting and anguished acknowledgments of weakness and evil. Finally, he might wonder whether *confession* was quite the proper word to describe such remarks as, "I am this way because. . . ."

The realm of causation is treacherous ground for a man interested in the truth about himself. Although it is certainly probable that most phenomena of this world, human and otherwise, do have causes of one sort or another, an absorption with the role of causation in human affairs may lead to an habitual reduction of any human event to its (postulated) cause. It is apparent how such reduction promises refuge to a man beset by the necessity to "confess": once he turns his attention to cause, his personal responsibility (whether he acknowledges this or not) is diminished, along with any undue stress or discomfort he may have felt in facing what he believes to be his absolute worst. No matter what scandalous detail about himself he may reveal, he follows such revelation with "I am this way because . . . ," and everyone relaxes. Given the customary forms of psychology and a close-knit society of colleagues all trained to abide by these forms, and given in addition the harrowing, threatening, and chaotic environment of a sanitarium for schizophrenia, it is hardly a wonder that the solace of causation persistently tempts these therapists and appears most seductive when they are speaking with one another about themselves and their lives with their patients. Even should a therapist's account of himself on such occasions include no direct reference to cause, his remarks are apt to lack that hesitant, hard-come-by quality that tends to characterize the statements of a man truly involved in making a moral confession.

Our visitor, as his stay in the sanitarium lengthened, might —depending on the degree of his disenchantment—soon find the atmosphere oppressive, sickly, somewhat like living in a hothouse where, in the midst of lush vegetation, the temperature was always too hot, the sunlight filtered and indirect, the humidity and fertility always controlled, with none of the accident of sudden cold or wind. Particularly as he listened to the therapists in conference, admonishing and even reassuring one another with countertransference interpretations, he might choose another image to describe the stifling effect on himself: a chamber of distorting mirrors, such as one finds in amusement parks, in which all that may be seen are reflections of reflections of reflections—of the psyches of the therapists. Failure, principally, but also the occasional therapeutic success finds its cause and its meaning, by default of

other sources of meaning, in the materials of countertransference, which constitutes a fashionable form of psychological
determinism among those who treat schizophrenia.

Much of the responsibility for this absorption with countertransference lies in the nature of schizophrenia itself, which is
a disorder consisting of a double failure in areas that might
loosely be called meaning and relation. The intellectual defect,
so strikingly displayed in the awkwardness with language, has
been variously described in studies of schizophrenic thinking.
Such civilized qualities as discretion, reticence, humor, judgment, and logic are poorly developed, if they are present at
all. In the imaginative realm, what we usually call the capacity
for metaphorical thinking is morbidly deficient, causing the
schizophrenic's understanding and perceptions, as well as his
efforts to communicate, to be uncomfortably literal. This
disability of imagination may be mistaken by the therapist for
the workings of the bared unconscious—as though the unconscious were not subject to refinement. Here, he is apt to
regard as symbol either what properly is not symbol at all, or
what could fairly be called only the rudiments of symbol. It
is as though the therapist imagined the schizophrenic to contain inside him a nonschizophrenic poet, who manipulated and
molded his symbolic utterances and gestures, concealing in
some inside pocket that texture of meaning that symbols may
achieve. However, it is more likely that this nonschizophrenic
poet, if he exists at all, resides not inside the patient, but in
the head of the therapist, who attributes to his patient's utterances a richness of meaning that is simply not deserved. I
should mention that there are certain desirable aspects to the
therapist's attribution of meaning to the verbal or gestural
productions of his schizophrenic patient; not only does the
patient need such imaginative assistance, if he is to recover,
but such an exalted view of his capacities also incites an enthusiasm for this work on both sides that urges its continuance

in the teeth of the discouragements that are intrinsic to the therapeutic situation.

Nevertheless, there is a hazard to this investiture. Should the therapist forget the degree to which he has supplied meaning to a patient unable to provide any for himself, he may come to regard the schizophrenic as a sort of oracle with whom he sits each day—a truly ragged oracle, untutored, unverbal, and naturally unappreciated, who has the rare power to cut through the usual hypocrisies and pretentions of ordinary life, thereby arriving at some purely human meaning. His illness now appears as an appropriate response to the impurities in the therapist's heart, even to the deceits and contradictions of the world in which he lives.

Take the example of a schizophrenic young man whose disagreeable habit—in his family's home as well as in the ward—was a thunderous clearing of the throat, often followed by spitting on the floor. We may guess how disruptive this habit was to ordinary conversation and how furious his father became when the young man chose the hour of his father's favorite television program for his most explosive performances. Some of us might even have commiserated with the father when, on one occasion, he angrily switched off the set and said, "One or the other, not both. Either I sit here and listen to you, or else you quiet down so that we can watch this program." It is not entirely unreasonable, I think, to regard this young man's carrying-on as a contemptuous and willful bit of self-assertion. On the other hand, if we had been closeted with him for many months and had come to regard him as an oracle, we might see his behavior as an appropriate social protest against the bourgeois dishonesties of his family life, of which television represented only one. Hocking and spitting might appear to be the only valid or truthful event that ever occurred in this family. When approached as an oracle, the schizophrenic seems not only more perceptive, but more "real," which helps to explain the therapist's growing attraction, even addiction, to the companionship of schizophrenic patients.

Whatever may be the real "real" life that our oracular patient provides, language is not one of its virtues. Nor, for that matter does it include those areas of knowledge or imagination that live through language: literature, history, philosophy, and so on. What tends to be celebrated is what is vaguely termed "the nonverbal," as though this were a department of gesticulation that need have no lively connection with language. Often accompanying the therapist's exaltation of the nonverbal may be an active intolerance toward, or even disparagement of, language. "Just words" will be a recurring phrase among those who share this view of language; it will suggest that words in general, any words, are crude and deceptive tools when compared to that superior, and at the same time more elemental, mode that dispenses with words altogether. Once the therapist embraces this view, not only does his own language, spoken or written, fail to develop, but he also finds it increasingly difficult to deal in a discriminating fashion with the spoken or written language of others. I have known several therapists who, after years with schizophrenic patients, gave up reading altogether—and not with shame, but proudly, as though they were glad to leave this brand of conformity behind them. What language they retained took on a pedantic, self-assertive quality that did little service to the development of their ideas, but seemed increasingly to resemble physical gesture.

Let me mention one further consequence of endowing the schizophrenic with oracular powers—a consequence (for the therapist) that has been implicit in what I have already said. Partly because he has helped anoint this oracle by supplying meanings that the oracle did not possess, partly because the work itself has required him to assert meanings with an assurance he himself did not at first possess, and partly because his audience was both captive and unresponsive, the therapist, by virtue of the prolonged apprenticeship he has served in the most self-indulgent kind of self-expression, may gradually be led toward both the posture and, ultimately, the belief that he, too, is an oracle—well-dressed rather than ragged, affluent rather than impoverished, legally sane rather than clinically schizophrenic, and yet possessed of the same charismatic power to grasp the real truth in any situation, regardless of what his intellectual or educational limitations may be. With the assumption of this toga, that dramatic room-filling quality to which I have referred will have unfolded to full bloom. Though mad in that private sense in which he seems to have fallen away from his own particular direction in life and to have lost all relation to the shy, studious, thoughtful young man he may once have been, he will appear eminently wise, although possibly rather florid and eccentric, to those younger therapists whom he will train in the intricacies of the therapeutic life with schizophrenia.

We can now return to that most important aspect of our subject: the issue of the connection between relation and will. I believe that this unholy conspiracy characterizes, in an important sense, the behavior of both therapist and schizophrenic, not only in their relationship with each other, where it achieves its most dramatic form, but also, and equally importantly, in the relationship of each to his world, to all others, and to himself. In spite of the fact that the intellectual life of the schizophrenic is as fearfully impoverished as his capacities for relation with others, we must assume that he is still human enough to hunger for relation and, should it be even fleetingly achieved, to dread and to be enraged by its loss. In such an extreme state, much of his delusional and hallucinatory life will either reach for consummation, even glory, or else proclaim his repudiation of such a possibility with a web of corroborating, though fantastic, details. By his impoverishment, he is reduced in his attempts at relation, or in his repudiation of relation (and often the two are intermingled), to what I choose to call his isolated will—or willfulness, if we define it as *Webster's* does, namely, that state in which one is governed by will without yielding to reason; obstinate; perverse; stubborn. It is a most important part of schizophrenia, and one that has been relatively neglected in the literature, though aspects of it have been considered under other categories. I would say that willfulness not only accounts for much of the schizophrenic's behavior, but authors a great deal of his delusional material. Without the assistance of the imagination, the will invents in its own image; this means that the will contrives plots in which will is pitted against will, its subject matter being, roughly, power. In delusion, the willful one may be an outside agent and the schizophrenic his victim, but, regardless of who is villain and who victim, the plot represents a crude example of what Yeats called "the will trying to do the work of the imagination." To some extent power *is* a real and ubiquitous motive in the world. Thus, if the therapist is adept at supplying texture and meaning to the plot, it is easy to see how he may come to endow his schizophrenic patient with an oracular vision of how power controls and corrupts the affairs of all men.

Willfully, then, the schizophrenic grasps at, and withdraws from, relation—sometimes simultaneously. Sullivan once remarked that he thought that, with the exception of periods of panic, the schizophrenic's life with others was largely hysterical in character. Although my understanding of hysteria is quite different from Sullivan's, I think I know what led him to this observation. It was, I suspect, the violent, flamboyant, impulsive, often explosive and destructive quality of the schizophrenic's social movements that reminded him of hysteria. In this regard we should remind ourselves that one or two of the first hysterics Freud and Breur studied would today be diagnosed as schizophrenic. To take but one example: the muteness of a particular schizophrenic may have originated in panic, when talk led him into such terrifying confusion about reality that his distress, instead of being relieved, was not only perpetuated but intensified. But as his panic subsides, his muteness may become, and remain, a willful refusal to talk, in response to what he regards as the demand to talk being made on him by those about him. Reduced to his own will, the schizophrenic perceives himself continually assailed by the willful demands of others. Examples of schizophrenic willfulness, whether or not they had their antecedents in panic, and despite the often confusing nature of their delusional elaboration or justification, are numerous: the refusal to eat, waxy inflexibility or the refusal to move, untidiness and nakedness, even smearing. All these may be willful responses to what seems to the schizophrenic to be willfulness on the part of those responsible for his care. Most of these examples are expressions of rejection of relation, but it should be said that the schizophrenic's sexual attempts to force intimacy can be equally willful, as with Dr. Fromm-Reichmann's masturbating patient, seeming almost assaultive in their grotesque lack of the nuances that usually assist the life of affection.

Not until the willfulness of the schizophrenic is recognized can it be understood why the therapeutic life with schizophrenia is such a bloodcurdling affair, its melodrama underscored by screaming invective, physical grappling of a brutal order, and all manner of obscenity. Even the mildest, most unassuming therapist, if he continues in this work, will soon find himself hurled into an arena where will is pitted bodily against will. He may even come to count himself fortunate to have this semblance of relation, no matter how degraded, instead of none at all, which is his more frequent lot.

It is hardly surprising that the more violent forms of the therapy of schizophrenia should seem to be life in the raw, making all ordinary civilized existence trivial by comparison. But the problem for the therapist is more serious than this. Whether he is locked in frantic physical encounter with his patient, or else trying, through monologue, to breach his patient's muteness, he is thrown back on his own isolated will in his efforts to provoke relationship. Even in defeat, he may resort to a silence that is as willful as the silence of his patient. It can be said that both therapist and patient have a will to relation and a relationship of wills. But this is a rather reckless use of the word "relation." Relation, understood in any decent sense, cannot be willed: it happens or it doesn't happen, depending on what human qualities are brought to the event: honesty, imagination, tact, humor, and so on. By contrast, the willful encounter—a far cry from the chancy and fleeting mutuality that occurs from time to time between people, and that we designate by the honorable term "relation"—will have a special binge-like excitement, even though its center is hollow. Its intensity is of the moment; unlike friendship, when the moment vanishes, little remains. This is the reason that the addictive possibilities of this therapeutic life are considerable. (In this regard it is no accident that two of the best-known therapists in the field have attempted to give ontological status to the experience of loneliness.) As the therapist returns again and again to the excitements of this drama of wills that passes for relation, he becomes increasingly impatient of relation, although it is unlikely he will cease believing, and asserting, that the capacity for relation is his special power. Gradually, but not casually, he develops into an apostle of relation who can no longer abide relation. It is an unhappy fact that when, through drugs or life-situation, one finds more and more scope for willfulness, those other human qualities I have mentioned are not merely held in abeyance, but fall into the atrophy of disuse. And, with such atrophy, the ordinary amenities of the world become not only no longer sustaining, but actually disturbing, making recourse to the drug ever more compelling. As the therapist continues to will what cannot be willed, those attributes of character to expand and harden will be precisely those public, self-assertive gestures that are unfaithful to the person he might have become.

Schizophrenia, of course, is not contagious. In no way do I mean to suggest that the therapist, by virtue of prolonged exposure to schizophrenia and of the possibility of his eventual addiction to intimate association with its victims, actually succumbs to this particular infection and turns schizophrenic himself. He does not become schizophrenic; but, as I have said, he tends to become something other than the person he is, or was, or was meant to be. It has been my intention in this discussion to propose that the curious nature of the person he *does* become may best be understood as a particular and personal, and characteristic, response to that particular disorder of human potentiality that is schizophrenia.

10

PERFECTIBILITY AND THE PSYCHOANALYTIC CANDIDATE

When I was first admitted to psychoanalytic training twenty years ago, I assembled with four other colleagues to hear a sermon by one of the senior training analysts. All that remains with me of that somber occasion is a picture of this learned man standing above us, grasping the top of a rickety folding chair. He looked quite devout to me as, with eyes lowered, he rocked himself back and forth and thus admonished us: "Though you have been accepted for psychoanalytic training, you are not psychoanalysts. Should you be asked, identify yourselves merely as psychiatrists. And, by no means are you to designate the work you do as psychoanalysis." Between him and me there seemed to be an impossible gulf—not only of esoteric skills and knowledge, but, more important, of a quality of being that I assumed was the most important reward of this long period of training I was yet to undergo. His admonition remains with me to this day. When pressed, I find it hard to designate my insufficient person as that of a psychoanalyst, and I feel I am taking some advantage of the truth when I identify my work as psychoanalysis. My experience cannot be too different, say, from that of proselytes of the Catharist heresy in the twelfth century, who were divided into the Pure and the Impure. So difficult was the attainment of Purity, that this spiritual distinction often did not arrive until the moment of last rites.

This particular heresy, with its promise of earthly perfection, provoked the church into the first mass slaughter in Western history. If psychoanalysis is a variety of heresy, it will not, I think, result in genocide at the hands of the mother church. What I shall be more concerned with in these remarks is the effects of our heresy, if that is what it is, on its celebrants.

Let me say quickly that our heresy, although resembling its predecessors in its gnostic nature, is a peculiarly modern and secular variety, and, unlike earlier heresies within the church, the heretical portion of its doctrine is largely unacknowledged. Stripped of the usual scientific qualifications, it might be expressed in this manner: *however rarely the goal of perfection may be achieved, man is a creature who is, nonetheless, psychologically perfectible, by virtue of either the early and happy accident of childhood or the later and unhappy necessity of psychoanalysis.* (In keeping with such a theory, of course, the word "accident" must be understood as a rather condescending metaphor for something that is in no way accidental. The idea of perfectibility is as dependent on some form of determinism as it is disdainful of the chaotic freedom that would permit someone to have an "accidental" sort of childhood. Once perfectibility is postulated, its logical mechanisms fit together to forge a deterministic, chance–proof continuity, extending its exclusive claim over past and future alike. Tucked away in this chain of causation is one of determinism's most logically baffling, yet favorite, propositions: if the determining factors are identified and understood, they may be manipulated; this results in the interesting phenomenon of a logically lawful and impersonal determinism, subject to will.) No sensible psychoanalyst would confess agreement with the doctrine of perfectibility, when so nakedly stated as it is above; yet I would suggest that, covertly, it accounts for many of our professional miseries, particularly during our training.

Unlike any other profession I know, with the possible exception of the priesthood, psychoanalysis places a double burden on its candidates; not only must they acquire psychoanalytic skills and knowledge—a difficult enough task in itself—but they must, in addition, undergo a lengthy period of psychoanalytic therapy, which at once calls into question what they had previously taken for granted—namely, their characters—while promising, or stipulating, something variously called growth, or maturity, as the outcome of this experience. Thus, at the same time that they are asked to address themselves wholeheartedly to complex theoretical and clinical problems, they are beset through their own psychoanalysis by a degree of self-absorption that in some ways quite opposes the pursuit of their subject matter. And, the reverse dilemma is equally burdensome. At the same time that they are asked to address themselves wholeheartedly to disorganizing and reforming their own characters, they are prompted, by their didactic studies, to a scientific inspection of that very process. The difficulty of being both subject and student at once produces a disturbing self-consciousness that affects both aspects of their training. Whereas it is quite true that the theories of psychoanalysis cannot be usefully learned and understood as though they were propositions of chemistry, in that they must to some extent be personally grasped and subjectively imagined, the degree of often painful self-involvement and crippling self-doubt that attend one's own analysis are not always helpful partners to imagination. Conversely, while runaway subjectivity interferes with analytic progress, and some "objective" perception of one's self and one's feelings is essential, this requirement is seldom served by the rather unnaturally and irrelevantly detached self-scrutiny that absorption with theoretical formulae invites. Achieving some objectivity toward oneself and assigning scholarly and hyphenated labels to one's symptoms are far from identical operations; scientific objectivity is not, if I may be didactic, subjective objectivity; it is, in fact, its opposite and its enemy when the two are confused.

If my recollection of the first days of training is correct, the onslaught of theory and personal analysis made me depressingly aware of my limitations as a human being, whatever my claims to scholarship might have been, and this new self-consciousness widened the personal gulf even further between me and my teachers. Unlike graduate students in other fields, I was oppressed, not only by my ignorance in matters psychoanalytic, which is natural enough for a student, but also by my growing sense of plain human insufficiency. So deeply impressed was I by this new science, that I believed every gesture or statement I might make before my colleagues and teachers clearly exposed my particular imperfections to the scrutiny of all. It did not occur to me at this stage that my absorption with myself might be matched by a similar self-absorption in my fellows, or, indeed, that the vigilance of their watch over me might not equal my own. The thought that only my own naïveté made me think myself so transparent was a stranger to my mind. Dutiful to the discipline of my field, I was so attentive to motive at the expense of content that I often failed to respond, or even listen, to the remarks of others, as if their manifest meaning were not of any consequence compared to the motives that might be inferred from the fact, context, or style of their delivery. Doubting, in turn, that my own statements would be received with a courtesy I myself withheld, like all my fellow students I guarded my own speech closely for the motives it might reveal. Although we students attended the open meetings of the society, we huddled together mutely, except for our whispered comments to each other, and prayed we would not be called upon to express—and expose—ourselves.

One comfort we found for our feeling of intimidation, that must have been miserable for our nonpsychoanalytic friends, was to load our speech with bits of jargon. Such jargon gave us the sweet and illicit thrill of using the secret tongue of our new fraternal order. More important, though, we used jargon in order to make some brash, half-humorous, and hopefully honest introductory statement about our pathology, before getting on with what we had to say. Naming, or even bragging about, our imperfections in this seemingly objective fashion somewhat lightened our growing awareness of the impossible distance we had yet to travel. Sometimes we would think in despair, "Well, maybe this is the way it is; maybe maturity is nothing more than the ability to name one's sins; maybe that other goal is pure fiction." Still, as a dark monument to the power of so noble a fiction, if it be fiction, or to the priority of even unknowable fact, if it be fact, that other goal towered before us, and we labored in its shadow.

How sharp and painful was the stirring of that other goal in our hearts was revealed by our endless and relentless appetite for gossip about our elders in the society. Every new instance of adultery, drunkenness, or divorce among our teachers was savored as evidence that they hadn't achieved perfection after all. We simply could not hear often enough of the ways in which they had failed as human beings. However, such is the misty nature of our theory and our ideal of perfection; it was always possible to interpret even their failures as manifestations of the freedom that would come with perfection. When we said to each other, "Well, they're only human," and replied to each other, "Of course!" we may have been trying to say that perfection is perhaps not a matter of being human, but is beyond the human, and that a human being who has achieved this exalted state is automatically permitted a more casual—i.e., free, or irresponsible—relationship to his lingering humanness. Failing to persuade ourselves of this unlikely but seductive notion, we might have said more truthfully: "They may be, even as we are, only human, but they ought to be more." Certainly we knew *we* ought to be more, even if perfection had to be pursued by lifelong analysis. And for a few of us, it did.

There were periods when we quite resigned ourselves to the bleak impossibility of ever being fully analyzed, only to be rudely aroused by news that one of the group was to be made a member. "Why him?" we would cry. Summoning our nerve, we would appeal to reason in our teachers: "Look, I'm perfectly well aware that I have plenty of problems, but as far as I can see he has just as many as I have. Maybe more. If you're going to admit *him*, then what about *me*?" I shall spare you both the details of this debate, and the ensuing conversations among the candidates about the corruption of that organization that is psychoanalysis. Nor shall I dispute the truth contained in our criticism of the power operations of this society. It is simply a fact that, unlike members of other professions, psychoanalysts of whatever theoretical creed show an astonishing capacity to organize themselves intricately into local and national societies. Freud and his initial group were a slovenly and eccentric lot compared with his epigones, who have hatched committees out of committees, courses out of courses, rules out of rules. But, of course, the founders of psychoanalysis were a vanguard group, intoxicated by the possibility of a whole new approach to psychology. They certainly were not yet possessed by heretical strivings toward perfection, even though their writings were beginning to develop both explicitly and implicitly that image of perfection that now plagues us all. Various explanations have been offered for the mushrooming of requirements for graduation, most of them containing some element of truth. In addition, I would suggest that the ideal itself, essentially subjective in its claims on us, had to be reformulated objectively—even numerically—since numerical requirements, unlike the subjective ideal, can be fulfilled. But, because the ideal remains covert, and unrealized, external standards proliferate unceasingly, in an attempt to capture the ideal objectively. If such proliferation continues, graduation—as in the Catharist heresy—will one day come only with last rites.

Let me now return briefly to the harsh disillusionment that follows the discovery—even if it has been anticipated—that graduation is not equivalent to perfection of self. As I have already suggested, one recourse to this discovery is cynicism, perhaps even nihilism. Obviously, we say to ourselves, there is no idealism here: training is simply a matter of taking the required courses, accumulating the requisite number of hours of personal analysis and supervision, and, finally, making sure that the powers that be are not offended by personal or theoretical eccentricity. In fact, perhaps graduation is a measure, not so much of our achievement, as of the despair and exhaustion of our teachers. When asked if we have finished our analysis, we must learn to say "yes," and then quickly qualify our answer with some vague assertion that, of course, there is more to do, and that we will, perhaps later on, return to analysis. Indulging our cynicism, we may play privately with such Machiavellian definitions as: "A fully analyzed person is a person who convincingly asserts to his group that he is fully analyzed." Such a cynical attitude, I would contend, is never firmly held: it is fleeting, and offers little solace for the more enduring sense of the discrepancy between one's actual self and the perfect self that is held to be possible.

It is fashionable to complain that candidates these days are far more conforming to middle-class values than were the candidates twenty years ago. In this complaint, it is suggested that Freud was too unbalanced to be accepted as a candidate today, that psychoanalytic institutions now prefer the well-behaved and amiable to the unruly gifted and disagreeable. I think there is truth to this observation, but I am not satisfied that this change comes merely from the increasing institutionalization of a movement that, in its beginnings at least, was more inspired and bohemian in nature. It seems to me more likely that, as an unacknowledged image of earthly psychological perfection settled in the minds of the majority of psychoanalysts, discontent with the actuality of the analyzed self chafed and mounted. Perfection was demanded, and yet it could not be grasped inwardly. Unable to be what was required of him, the candidate turned in desperation to dramatizing his possession of the well-being he could not possess, by assuming what he hoped were its outward manifestations and appearances. In this imitation of being that is behaving, he strove to create an illusion of so-called maturity, a style of life and statement that would persuade others that he actually had realized those psychological values that continued privately to elude him. A style of life so self-imposed and so at odds with being itself, will, by definition, be more trite and predictable than surprising.

Predictable, however, not only in its outward conformity, but also in the burden of its inward pain. When man believes in his perfectibility, he experiences his own real being almost as a disease, a fatal sickness whose cure—perfection—seems unattainable for himself, and whose tormenting symptoms can only partially be eased by the exchange of seeming for being.

When he measures himself, not by his acts, which may reveal what he *is*, but by his actions, his image of himself becomes external, objective, and turns for its definition to a psychology of behavior. And, we hardly notice that we have almost ceased to wonder what maturity, say, might subjectively feel like or be to the individual, since we now know so very much about what it looks like or does. Being, however, is not easily denied. Deception on such a grand scale as I have described, especially in those who are trained in self-scrutiny, is usually too large an order even for those with considerable talent for acting, so that no matter how convincing the candidate's efforts may be to others, to him they are the movements of misery. Every gesture he makes in imitation of the ideal (a role as recognizable as Hamlet, though requiring greater gifts) reminds him shamefully of his pretenses and painfully of his real limitations, that appear, in the shadow of the ideal, ever more huge and menacing. Thus does the noble dream of perfection make cynics of us all, destroying our infinite variety, reducing us to our facility for imitation, and rendering us despicable to ourselves.

Desire for self-improvement, striving after goals, aspiring toward an ideal—these ambitions were not suddenly thrust into human experience in the second half of the nineteenth century; they antedate modern psychology by several thousand years at least. Man has always measured himself against what he is not, but might become—his goals; and against what he can never become, but can move toward—his ideals. Throughout history, man has often been tyrannized by his own ambition, but his ideals—in their very nature—could not enslave him so long as he could recognize and acknowledge the impossible. Ideals in the pre-Freudian past usually concerned themselves with those distinctly human virtues that were central to man's definition of himself: discrimination, judgment, intelligence, taste, restraint, humility, imagination, to name but a few. The ideal—the perfection of any such virtue—was clearly beyond human reach, but its image penetrated the human sphere just deeply enough to illuminate a direction, a path toward ever greater exercise and refinement of virtue, a path with no point of arrival for man, that lay across the very center of his life. With the exception of the doctrines of a few religious heresies, little claim was made for the perfectibility of the total man. Man knew himself to be an imperfect creature, and his own imperfectibility was as essential to his definition of himself as were the sins that he committed, the temptations that raged in his heart, the virtues that he honored, the faith or hope that he cherished.

With the development of psychoanalysis at the turn of the century, a whole new body of psychological evidence and hypothesis, all proceeding exclusively from attention to psychological disorder or pathology, invigorated the perennial issue of what is human. In the sheer excitement of these discoveries and inventions, analysts tended to forget older sources of wisdom pertaining to the same question. Instead, as though they were the first citizens to arrive on this planet, they attempted to derive an entire way of life from their theories of pathology. The examples are legion. If authoritarian fathers produce neurotic children, children should be raised in co-operative nurseries away from parental pressures. If oral fixation leads to schizophrenia, then breast-feeding not only prevents schizophrenia, but furnishes the conditions for the development of a normal human being. If repressed hostility accounts for certain types of misery, then free expression of anger is evidence of maturity. In other words, when human virtue is the opposite of defect, absence of defect means presence of virtue. Complete absence of all defects means complete virtue, or—perfection. Virtues which are the absence of defects have very little relevance to any knowledge of virtue we may have that has come to us, not from psychology, but from other sources of information about what is human: history, literature, philosophy, religion, or our own experience—all of which have not only always recognized human imperfectibility, but have constantly warned man against the grave dangers of believing himself perfectible. The theories of psychoanalysis seem to tempt us to forget, or even to ignore, these warnings, offering us a promise and a plan for our own perfection. Nevertheless, we must remind ourselves that, though imperfect, we may still become whole. And should we succumb to the heresy of perfectibility, our tragedy will be that we defeat our potentiality for wholeness. Such heresy, however, does not rise inevitably from our doctrines, but captures us only when we use those doctrines to estrange us from all other knowledge of ourselves.

Acknowledgments

Chapter 1 was written for this book.

Chapter 2 originally appeared as "Will and Anxiety," *Review of Existential Psychology and Psychiatry*, 4 (Fall 1964), No. 3.

Chapter 3 originally appeared as "I'm Sorry, Dear," *Commentary*, November 1964.

Chapter 4 originally appeared as "Despair and the Life of Suicide," *Review of Existential Psychology and Psychiatry*, 2 (Spring 1962), No. 2.

Chapter 5 originally appeared as "Will and Willfulness in Hysteria," *Review of Existential Psychology and Psychiatry*, 1 (Fall 1961), No. 3.

Chapter 6 originally appeared as "Faces of Envy," *Review of Existential Psychology and Psychiatry*, 1 (Spring 1961), No. 2.

Chapter 7 originally appeared as "Martin Buber and Psychiatry," *Psychiatry*, 19 (1956), No. 2. Reprinted by special permission of The William Alanson White Psychiatric Foundation, Inc.; copyright held by the Foundation.

Chapter 8 originally appeared as "The Therapeutic Despair," *Psychiatry*, 21 (1958), No. 1. Reprinted by special permission of The William Alanson White Psychiatric Foundation, Inc., copyright held by the Foundation.

Chapter 9 originally appeared as "Schizophrenia and the Mad Psychotherapist," *Review of Existential Psychology and Psychiatry*, 2 (Fall 1962), No. 3.

Chapter 10 originally appeared as "Perfectibility and the Psychoanalytic Candidate," *Journal of Existential Psychiatry*, 3 (Winter 1963), No. 11.

Index

Abraham, Karl, 132 n.
absolute power, in hypnosis, 104–105
abstinence, sexual, 53
acting out, 110
action, postponement of, 23
Adler, Alfred, 120
Adler, Mortimer, 3
adultery, 52, 69
"Age of Anxiety," 47
"Age of Disordered Will," 48
aggression, 102; envy and, 120; as will, 31
alcohol, despair and, 91; hysteria and, 110–111; and sexual frustration, 51–52
alienation, 33
anecdotalism, obsessive, 177
anger, free expression of, 218
Anna Karenina (Tolstoy), 12–15
anxiety, 102, 171; ambiguity of, 35; basic, 35; bodily response in, 33, 47; as categorical abstraction, 34; as conflict of will, 42; defined, 32, 42; drugs and, 48; existential, 36, 47; versus fear, 45; "helpless" nature of, 47; inner, 45; as solicitous or earnest desire, 36; Sullivan on, 36–43; synonyms for, 32–33; will and, 26–50

anxiety theory, dissatisfaction with, 32
Auden, W. H., 8
Augustine, St., 3, 54
automanipulative approach, 58–60

Beerbohm, Max, 118
behaviorism, 139
being, "radical rejection" of (Marcel), 93
bodily estrangement, 56
bodily response, in anxiety, 33, 47; in orgasm, 58–62
body, knowledge of, 54–55; as natural object, 71; as "objectification of will" (Schopenhauer), 116
breast envy, 129
breast-feeding, 218
Breuer, Josef, 206
Brill, A. A., 160 n.
Buber, Martin, vii, 8 n., 9 n., 54, 76, 80, 96, 156, 167, 181; psychoanalysis and, 131–154
Burnham, Donald L., 148
Butler, Samuel, 30

Camus, Albert, 82
Catharist heresy, 210, 215
causality, 32, 199–200
charisma, 187
charity, 171

child, *I–Thou* relation in, 141–142
Christ, imitation of, 166
coitus, artificial, 61 n.
communication, 144
consensual validation, 144
countertransference, 191, 199, 201
counter-will, 6–7

Dante Alighieri, 118
death, "cheating" of by suicide,
    96
dependence, as will, 31
depression, 83
despair, 31, 42; suicide and, 76–98;
    therapeutic, 155–183
determination, will as, 4
determinism, psychic, 35
distress, anxiety as, 32
doctor–patient relationship, 180
Dora case (Freud's), 27, 30, 99–
    102, 106–107, 163–164
Dostoyevsky, Fyodor, 6, 30, 50, 84,
    86
double bind, 198
dread, 33
Dru, Alexander, 131, 182 n.
drugs, dependence on, 48; despair
    and, 91; sexual frustration and,
    51–52
Dyer's Hand, The (Auden), 8

ego, 33
ejaculatio praecox, 71
Eliot, T. S., 83, 87, 155
emulation, envy and, 123
Enneads, The, 9 n.
envy, 31, 80; alienating effect of,
    122; definitions of, 118–119;
    greed and, 124, 129; jealousy
    and, 124–126; penis, 129; rivalry
    and, 127
erotic life, dialogue in, 54; study
    of, 71

erotic man, 147
experience, will and, 25

fact, versus feeling, 138
Fairbairn, W. Ronald D., 132 n.
Fall, The (Camus), 82
fear, anxiety as, 33; outer, 45
feeling, versus fact, 137
female masturbation, 58, 74
Ferenczi, Sándor, 121
Flaubert, Gustav, 30
Fliess, Robert, 99
foreplay, 71
Four Quartets (Eliot), 83
free association, 138, 169
freedom, versus isolated will, 48;
    psychological, 174; suicide as,
    90; will and, 9–10, 48
"free will," 10
Freud, Sigmund, 27–28, 30, 89, 99,
    105, 114, 121, 132, 155–156, 206;
    on art, 162; on Dora case, 100–
    102, 106–107, 163–164; on homo-
    sexuality, 165; on libidinal drives,
    140; on philosophy, 160
Friedman, Maurice S., vii, 137 n.,
    144
fright, 33
frigidity, 64, 71
Fromm-Reichmann, Frieda, 149–
    150, 152, 191–193, 206

Gawel, Mary Ladd, 161 n.
genetic fallacy, 139
genital character, 131–132
God, existence of, 50, 87, 89; and
    I–Thou relation, 136; self-will
    of, 90
Goldstein, Kurt, 34, 42
Goncharov, Ivan A., 30
greed, envy and, 124, 129
grief, 42
Groddeck, Georg, 192

guilt, despair and, 96; memory of, 80; need and, 175; as will, 31

Hamlet (Shakespeare), 159
Herberg, Will, 157
Hobbes, Thomas, 120
homosexuality, 114, 164–165
Horace (Quintus Horatius Flaccus), 118
Horney, Karen, 35
hostility, repressed, 218
Huckleberry Finn (Mark Twain), 113
human condition, psychiatry and, 151
humility, 83
hypnosis, 104
hysteria, 27; aestheticism of, 113–115; as disorder of the will, 103–105; emotionality of, 110; as female disorder, 114; Freud's case of, *see* Dora case; ignorance and, 112; manner of, 107; passion and, 117; sexual activity and, 102; will and willfulness in, 99–117

Ibsen, Henrik, 30
identification, 33
ignorance, in hysteria, 112
I–It relation, 134–147
imagination, memory and, 21; will and, 16–17, 19–22, 44
impulsivity, 110
individual, in literature, 29–30
inferiority, as will, 31
intellect, will and, 44, 115
I–Thou relation, 10, 134–147

jargon, use of, 213
jealousy, 124–126
Jewish philosophy and theology, 154
Johnson, Virginia E., 61

Jones, Ernest, 163 n.
Jung, Carl Gustav, 133 n.

Kafka, Franz, 131
Kierkegaard, Sören, viii, 8, 79, 88, 120, 181, 183, 195
King Lear (Shakespeare), 159
Kinsey, Alfred, 56, 72
Kinsey Report, 72
Kirillov (*The Possessed*), on suicide, 86–91
Klein, Melanie, 198
knowledge, human, 152
Krook, Dorothea, 54

"Lady of the Laboratory," 62–69
Lawrence, D. H., 56
Leonardo da Vinci, 29
Lewis, C. S., 51
libido, 30, 109, 140
"life of suicide," defined, 77–78
listening, psychoanalysis and, 145; speech and, 20
literature, concern of with individual, 29–30
love, orgasm as, 56–58, 147
lust, 54

MacKenna, Stephen, 9 n.
manual manipulation, orgasm and, 58
Marcel, Gabriel, 76, 78, 86, 93
Masters, William H., 56–61, 65
masturbation, 58, 69–70, 73–74; encouragement in, 192–193, 206
May, Rollo, 34, 42
megalomania, 140
melancholy, 42
melodrama, psychotic, 150
Melville, Herman, 104
memory, of former speech, 19–20; imagination and, 21; will and, 16 n., 22
Mesmer, Franz Anton, 104

metaphysical thought, suicide as starting point of, 76, 86
morality, ideal of, 166; psychoanalysis and, 153; sex and, 54–55; will and, 23
moral situation, meaning of, 112
mother–child relation, 140–141
motive, will and, 31

narcissism, 140
neurosis, 73
Nietzsche, Friedrich, 5, 50
Nietzschean will, 7, 90
nonverbal behavior, 203

Oblomovism, 3
obscenity, in schizophrenia, 206
obsessive anecdotalism, 177
omnipotence, 167
omniscience, 160–161, 167
onanism, 69; *see also* masturbation
Onasander, 118
oral fixation, 218
orgasm, clitoral and vaginal, 73; idealization of, 75; love as, 56–58, 147; through manipulation, 58–60, 67; movies of, 58–60; "perfect," 69; simultaneous, 56–58, 73–75

parataxic relation, 144
parochialism, 26–27
participant observation, 144
"participation," need for, 82
Pascal, Blaise, 8
patient–therapist relation, in schizophrenia, 207
penis, artificial, 61 n.; clitoris and, 73
penis-envy, 129
perfection, guilt and, 175; striving for, 213–214
perfectibility, concept of, 209–218
Perry, Helen Swick, 161 n.

philosophy, as "illusion," 160
Plato, 118
"playing God," 160–161
pleasure, power and, 55
Plotinus, 9 n.
poet, schizophrenic, 201
pornography, 68, 109–110
Possessed, The (Dostoyevsky), 6, 50, 84, 86
power, illusion of, in hypnosis, 104; as will, 31
procrastination, 23
projection, 33
prudery, 71–72
pseudo-*Thou*, 146–147
psychiatry, human condition and, 151; reductive, 133
psychic determinism, 35
psychoanalysis, Buber and, 131–154; character defects in analyst, 213–215; counter-will in, 6–7; double bind in, 211; hysteric patient in, 114; listening in, 145; morality and, 153; sexology and, 71; will as residue of, 28–29; *see also* hysteria; psychotherapy
psychoanalytic candidate, perfectibility of, 209–218
psychological category, 36
psychology, as exact science, 179; will therapy in, 5
psychotherapist, "mad," 184–208; "will" to become, 40–41
psychotherapy, despair of, 85; Freudian, 155–156, 161–162; of schizophrenia, 167–168, 173, 178–180, 184–208; will and, 27
psychotic melodrama, 150

Rank, Otto, 5–6
rationalism, 25, 158
reconciliation, craving for, 80
regression, 33